To Bruce

Best Wishes

[illegible]

8 · 7 · 98

India Revisited

The Golden Vision

by

Brian Holdich

By the same author
My Indian Journey

First published in Great Britain in 1998 by
Brian's Books (B.W. Holdich),
4 Elm Close,
Market Deeping,
Peterborough,
Cambs.
PE6 8JN

First published in 1998
ISBN 0 952 1017 1 8 (Paperback)
India Revisited

British Library cataloguing-in-publication data.
A catalogue record of this book is available from the British Library.

Printed and bound by Peter Spiegl & Co.,
6 St. George's Street,
Stamford,
Lincolnshire.
PE9 2BL

I dedicate this book to the memory of the four Ursuline sisters from Belgium who first arrived in the great sub-continent of India in 1901, and whose work is carried on today by a very special group of women.

Foreword

Brian can be found most weeks in Church at the 8am celebration of Holy Communion. His Christian faith has been a motivating factor behind his fascination for India and its poor.

Following his first trip to India he raised large sums of money for his adopted school and ever since has longed to return. I must confess that I urged caution, worried for his health and safety. I was also concerned that, in their desperation, some of the people he has helped were urging him to more and more major projects, including the unrealistic building of a fully-equipped hospital. Perhaps, I thought, our "Mr Brian" as he is known in India was believed to be a multi-millionaire or a business tycoon instead of the retired "man from the Pru" who had taken up their cause by speaking to innumerable small groups. Fortunately as it happens, he ignored my fears and went ahead with his longed-for return trip. The new encounters and experiences he has had are just as fascinating as the first and I am sure you will enjoy reading about them.

"Mr Brian" always writes from the heart and tells us of his innermost thoughts. There is humour and tragedy, the sheer joy of living and the despair of poverty, all the many and profound contrasts that a journey to India brings the traveller who is prepared to meet its people and be accepted by them, as Brian has.

This book is not simply a travel guide and is not designed for tourists. It is designed for those who want to gain a real insight into the lives of the people of India and, with Brian, want to do something to help.

Derek Earis
Rector
St Guthlac's Church, Market Deeping

Acknowledgments

It is with much appreciation that I thank, most sincerely, the following people, who have helped me with the publication of this book. First, I graciously thank Derek Earis, the Rector of St. Guthlac's Church, Market Deeping, for contributing the foreword. I would like to express enormous gratitude to Jan Dekker, who word-processed everything I wrote. The telephone was constantly in use between us, with me making constant alterations to the manuscript. My thanks also to Geoff Chambers, who checked the proofs before publication. I must thank, once again, my printers, Peter Spiegl & Co., of Stamford. After the success of my last book, I was unlikely to be looking for a different printer. I would like to thank the Liverpool Daily Post & Echo for sending me a photograph of the Everton and Scotland footballer Alex Young, "The Golden Vision", and for giving me permission to use it in the book.

I am indebted to the late Mother Teresa of Calcutta for allowing me to meet her again. I'm particularly grateful to Balaram. This Calcutta taxi driver's knowledge of that city was better than any tourist guide's. Also, I don't think I would have ventured into what is probably the biggest slum area in India without him by my side. The hospitality I was given by Dr Anjan K. Kar in that slum was absolutely wonderful. My warmest appreciation goes to him. Special thanks go to Albina Kujur's family, who, in the very heart of the Indian countryside, gave me such an extraordinary welcome. Finally, my wholehearted gratitude to all those brides of Christ, the Ursuline sisters of Bihar, who are spread throughout the wilds of that state. Without the love and protection these Catholic nuns gave me, this book could never have been written.

Contents

Acknowledgements
Foreword
Author's Preface i

1 Heathrow Heartbreak 1
2 Feelings 8
3 Return to Tongo 37
4 Sister Bernadette's Dream 55
5 The Heart of India 65
6 A Cry for Help 74
7 Bihar Babies 83
8 The Divine Sisters 95
9 Miracles 127
10 A Train Passage to Calcutta 142
11 Survival on the Streets 163
12 The Golden Vision 178

Author's Preface

"It is trite that one half of the world knows not how the other half lives. Who can say what sores might be healed, what hurts solved, were the doings of each half of the world's inhabitants understood and appreciated by the other."

Mahatma Gandhi

You would be surprised at the number of people who have said to me on more occasions than I care to remember: "I couldn't possibly visit India because I would hate to see all that dreadful poverty." I usually reply by telling them that one either likes the country or one does not. There are no half measures with India. One can either come back from a holiday there having enjoyed it immensely and saying it's the most wonderful experience one has ever had, or one can say bluntly "I hated it". India has that affect on people. Love it or hate it, a Westerner will never know until they have seen India. It is usually the poverty that turns people against it. The reason is simply that millions upon millions of people in the Indian subcontinent live in conditions well below any notion of acceptability used in the West. But me, I love the country because it really is a land of fantasy, dreams, colour and intrigue.

It stretches some 1,269,346, square miles and at the last census in 1991 the population was 846,302,688 making it the largest democracy in the word. The majority, 82.6 per cent, are Hindu, and the official language is Hindi, with New Delhi the capital. It is divided into 26 states and is a country where in some states law and order leave a lot to be desired. It is, incidentally, among the 10 most corrupt nations on Earth. Whether one loves it or hates it, one can certainly never forget it. It's been said that India can change a person. People having actually said that after visiting India they have never been the same again. Please believe me when I say it can leave a deep impression on a person. It had such an affect on me and I know it definitely changed me. It left such an overwhelming impression on me that I wanted to help the country. And I also knew, when I first visited India in November 1991 for 22 stimulating days, that I would not rest until I had visited it again. Well, I have revisited India and this, my second book on the country, brings my whole Indian experience up to date.

Why, then, did India have such a deep and lasting affect on me? To take the story from the very beginning, I must mention why I visited it in the first place. The story really started in 1978, when I began sponsoring an eleven-year-old Indian girl whose name was Albina Kujur. Through my paying a very small monthly amount of money to the overseas charity ActionAid, the girl received an education. She lived in the village of Tongo in southern Bihar, which is in north-east India. Because of my sponsorship she was able to attend the Ursuline convent school for girls in the village of Tongo. She was born into a low-caste Indian family who lived in one of the poorest areas of the world, where there is an ongoing cycle of misery from which there is no escape. Her parents were peasant farmers relying totally on the erratic rains for their very survival. Without the rains, and particularly the monsoon, there is starvation. It's as simple as that. We in the West only read of such things. Illiteracy is common, malnutrition is widespread and disease and early death are very much part of daily life. This was the world that Albina Kujur was born into. Little did I think, back in 1978, that I would be going to India just to meet her.

For over 10 years I sponsored this girl. Letters were exchanged between us and I knew she was no ordinary girl. Even though she was born into appalling poverty she had ambition. Not for her an arranged marriage. No, she wanted to attend college and become a schoolteacher. She wanted, if it was at all possible, to escape the sheer misery of being born into a lower-caste family in the Indian countryside, which is generally a passport to a miserable existence. You will read many times in this book of the caste system and the unfairness of it. The history of the caste system stems from many centuries ago when the Aryan tribes moved down from the north west and formed the basis of the great Hindu religion. The Aryan peoples had a three-tier social system of warriors, priests and common people and these were the origins of the caste system in Hinduism, which still exists today. Caste dictates the work you do, who you marry and even who you eat with. A fourth caste, known as the untouchables, was added later. They lead a horrid life as the outcasts of Indian society. If there is a hell on earth, it is theirs to endure. Such is the caste system in India. The upper-class Indian even feels he could be contaminated by contact with those lower down. The sheer snobbery, or should I say discrimination - unfair treatment of a person based on prejudice - ensures that well over 80 per cent of India's huge population lives a life that is, largely, dreadfully poor. Albina Kujur, her roots in the lower caste, faced such an existence.

So, on November 8, 1991 I flew to meet Albina, but while in India I wanted to see as much of it as possible. I toured New Delhi, I visited the Taj Mahal in the city of Agra and I stayed in Calcutta for nearly a week. While there I was fortunate to meet, of all people, Mother Teresa. During my travels I saw unforgettable squalor, the memory of which has never left me. How could human beings live in such filth, I asked myself continually. I was deeply shocked. I actually formed a kind of relationship with the street kids of Calcutta, who followed me about in droves. Seeing the smiles on their faces left me wondering what on earth they had to smile about, because theirs is an utterly miserable existence.

Arriving at Ranchi Airport, I was met by Albina and Sister Bernadette Tete, the senior school headmistress at Tongo. We travelled by Jeep into the very outback of India and through the very beautiful and colourful Bihar countryside. Finally, arriving in Tongo after many hours, I was welcomed by 15 Indian Ursuline sisters who run the convent school there. They teach 1,300 school children and it was also the school Albina attended. When I met her she was already halfway to that ambition of hers because she was studying to be a teacher at the Lohardaga Training College, which is 30 miles from Tongo. To my surprise these Ursuline sisters had a wicked sense of humour and I quickly struck up a rapport with them. The hospitality they gave me was truly wonderful. I knew I could never forget them and I knew that if I could repay them in any way then I would do so.

One day Sister Bernadette took me for a walk past part of the wall that encircled the school. A good half of this massive eight-foot brick and stone structure, which stretched well over half a mile, had been knocked down. Sister Bernadette asked me if I could help with the rebuilding of the wall by raising money on my return home to fund the repair work. The reason given for the repair was needed was that people from the village were evidently stealing the precious vegetables grown in the school garden. People were helping themselves to vegetables that were often the difference between life and death. Without them, the 400 boarders at the school just wouldn't survive because there wouldn't be anything for them to eat. I was also told that Tongo could one day become a dangerous area. The school was therefore crying out for protection and the

Ursuline sisters were getting increasingly nervous about there being so little security there. The children were in an extremely vulnerable position. Anyone could have walked in and done untold damage. With violence plainly on the increase throughout the state of Bihar, where terrible atrocities are being committed every day, the children had to be protected. This, therefore, was the task I'd been asked to carry out. From then on, it increasingly became an obsession to get that wall rebuilt. I had to think of various ways I could raise the necessary money, but where was I to make a start? I knew it wouldn't be easy raising money for an overseas cause, so when I arrived home from India at the end of November, 1991, I faced what was, without doubt, the greatest challenge of my life - and I knew I musn't fail.

By the Christmas of that year I had the idea that if I could write a book about my experiences in India, the proceeds could go towards the work on the wall. So I set about the job. I certainly had enough material because while I'd been in India I'd kept a diary documenting every single day's events. It was originally going to be for future generations of my family. Surely my meeting with Mother Teresa was worth writing about by itself and, as my trip was action-packed from start to finish, I was convinced I had a story to tell. As I was then still working full-time it wasn't easy to be writing a book at the same time and I quickly realised that the best time to write is when the mind is fresh. So, most mornings I was up at 6am to write for an hour before getting ready for a day's work. I must admit I did have grave doubts about whether the book would sell. I'd never written one before. I was really stepping into the unknown. It took me a year to write it, the eventual title being *My Indian Journey*. Because I'd never taken on such a mammoth task before, I thought my greatest asset in relation to the book's readers would be my sincerity and honesty. Above all, it had to appear genuine, so I wrote from the heart. The book would contain my feelings of India and certainly not anyone else's. I shall never forget the day when the first 500 books arrived from the printers, neatly parcelled in packages of 10. I stored them in my office at home. I would often look at them from my desk, wondering how on earth I was going to sell 500 books.

The book nevertheless started to sell reasonably well in the bookshops in the Peterborough area and I began to think of other ways of raising money to repair the wall, which, incidentally, was going to cost £4,000. One such method was to compete in the 1993 London Marathon. As I usually walk one marathon a year for some charity or other I did have certain reservations about asking people to sponsor me to repair a convent school wall in India. But I need not have worried because the response was fantastic. Just about everyone I asked to sponsor me did so, and I asked nearly 300 people. Through the good-heartedness of local people I was able to collect £1,400. Just think of it. That wall out in India meant nothing really to those sponsoring me. Surely I'd get some harsh replies while asking for money on the doorsteps. But nobody was rude to me. They just listened to what I had to say and they were only too pleased to help. The conclusion I came to was that when children are involved, which was undoubtedly the case in Tongo, people will respond positively no matter where in the world the money is actually going. Such generosity - how marvellous everyone was. I still can't forget it. Within weeks of collecting my sponsorship money a cheque was on its way to the Ursuline convent school in Tongo and the builders were able to start on the first phase of the repair work.

In my training programme for the London Marathon I pushed myself particularly hard. At times my legs felt so heavy that I thought I was trying to move railway sleepers as I strove to overcome the pain barrier. At other times I felt so good that I thought I could walk all day. I was determined to complete this marathon because of the number of people who had sponsored me. Also, I couldn't let the school down. There was so much at stake. In training I was walking at least 12 miles a day. The day of the marathon happened to be the hottest of the year by far and by the 19-mile mark I was struggling. I felt tired, my joints were aching and, believe me, while walking by the Embankment along the Thames the water can look so tempting when you are in that state. But the sense of occasion kept me going. As a walker, I was at the rear of the field with all the other charity walkers, many of them dressed in all sorts of strange outfits. The whole atmosphere was tremendous. For company I had a lady called Alice, who was 83 years of age. At times I couldn't keep up with her. The ecstasy of having that gold medal placed around my neck is something I'll never forget. Runners and walkers, many of them near exhaustion, were heard to say "this is the greatest day of my life" as they hit the finishing tape. I know that when I hit that tape it was a truly unforgettable feeling. I've been in two London Marathons since and the feeling was equally good. But that first time was special. I'd done it for the Tongo school.

Another money-raiser for the wall was my talk and slide show, as I called it. I sent hundreds of letters to different groups of people informing them that I was available to speak to them about *My Indian Journey*. I certainly was not an accomplished speaker, but I hoped I would improve through regular practice. Here again I thought I had something to offer because I had some lovely colourful slides of India. The response to those letters was staggering. I started speaking four years ago and in that time I've visited well over 100 different groups. I've spoken to Rotary clubs, Townswomen's Guilds, Women's Institutes, Probus clubs, Inner Wheel clubs, U3A groups, senior citizens, Mothers' Unions and countless others. Quite often I've spoken to three groups in a week. Once I did as many as six in a single week, travelling hundreds of miles by car. I've even spoken at a top-security prison. After being met by the chaplain at the main gates I was taken through numerous other iron gates, all of them unlocked and then locked behind me. I eventually found myself speaking to just seven inmates. The chaplain had told me they were all in for life, four of them being convicted murderers. Having spoken to them for about an hour, it was time for tea and biscuits and as the seven gathered around me it was like chatting to any ordinary group of people. One of them was in for armed robbery, which I didn't know until the chaplain told me later. On talking to this particular prisoner I got mildly excited when he said: "That wall, I'll send you some money to repair it." He said he would leave a cheque with the chaplain. Unfortunately I never did receive it. Wouldn't it have been interesting, though, if I'd received a cheque for, say, £25,000 from money this prisoner had salted away somewhere from his bank raid. Just think what money like that could have done for the Tongo school. Maybe this prisoner was a latter-day Robin Hood, stealing from the rich to give to the poor. As I drove home that evening I laughed to myself. Could this really happen, I thought. What should I have done if he had sent me some money. I need not have worried, though. My conscience was never put to the test.

Wherever I've spoken I've always taken a large supply of *My Indian Journey* books with me. At a U3A group in Sudbury in Suffolk I sold 22 books. There were 110 people there and as they were queuing up afterwards for a signed copy I couldn't sign them fast enough. That day was very productive. I returned home with £180, including 22 book sales, a donation, which I usually get from the groups I speak to, and the proceeds of the raffle. Next morning at home I answered the door to the postman, who had a registered letter from Sudbury. Enclosed was £100 in five crisp £20 notes. Obviously the lady who had sent them had been touched by what I'd said at the meeting. "Please get that wall repaired," she had written. That moment nearly brought tears to my eyes. The total altogether from Sudbury, therefore, was £280 for Tongo. Only recently at a Leicester NHS Retirement Fellowship meeting attended by 120 people I came away with nearly £200. The more people there are in the audience for me, the more the adrenaline flows and I'm sure I have improved my speaking and presentation skills. Of course, the more people who attend these meetings, the more books I can hopefully sell. People have even remarked that the book is undersold at its £5 price and asked me how I managed to keep it so low. People have not turned out in such large numbers everywhere, of course. On one occasion, just four people attended and one of those was my wife. Generally, though, the turnouts have been good. The visits have not been without their problems, however. With some of the elderly groups I have spoken to, for instance, it has been a real problem at times keeping them awake. Normally I speak for about an hour and for one particular group I deliberately cut my time down to half an hour. Even so, with the room being very warm and many of the audience being in their 90s (the oldest was 99), by the time I'd finished I'd actually sent about 30 people to sleep, with myself nearly included.

I've had some funny moments while on some of these visits. One lady shouted out: "For God's sake stop walking about. You're making me dizzy." I know I do have a bad habit of walking about while I'm speaking. Once, as I was trying to explain to a senior citizens group the problems of over-population faced by India, an elderly gentleman called out from the back of the hall, saying I should send a lorry-load of condoms to the subcontinent. Once, at a Women's Institute meeting - and, bless 'em, I've spoken to nearly 90 different groups - there were about 60 ladies present as I was describing how, with my shirt and vest off and my trousers half down, I was lying on my stomach on my bed while Sister Sushila, one of the Ursuline sisters at Tongo, massaged by back. This was happening because I'd hurt my back while in India. The same fate befell me on my second visit, too, incidentally. I told a hushed village hall that this sister had the most soothing hands imaginable. At this point I noticed some of the younger ladies sniggering amongst themselves. At the same time, some of the senior Women's Institute officials were shifting about rather uncomfortably in their front row seats. They must have wondered who this man was and what he was going to say next. At this precise moment a lady was heard to ask: "Did she massage anything else?" That remark brought the hall to uproar. There I was on stage facing 60 ladies in hysterical laughter. I wanted the floor to open up. I must have looked as red as a beetroot. I must admit that the massage episode has always brought a comment from the audience. Whoever that lady was, though, her timing was spot-on.

Another part of my talk and slide show which is usually good for a laugh is when I recall the time I feared I was eating rat's meat. I was sure that had been put on my plate the very first time I visited Albina's home. The poor peasant people in that part of Bihar are the tribe of Oron. Known as the rat eaters of India because they are so poor, that is exactly what they have to eat to avoid starvation. ActionAid had written to me of this when I first began sponsoring Albina. Rather than offend her family at a welcome party in my honour, I ate this meat. Not all of it, admittedly, but some of it, and as I was eating it I felt I was going to be sick. But at least I hadn't offended anyone. Some groups I've spoken to find this highly amusing, while others have a look of sheer astonishment and horror on their faces. "How could you possibly eat that?" they ask. I usually say that there was no escape, with 50 people in Albina's home watching my every move. Remember, I was a white man from England and, in all probability, no white person had ever entered that hut before. Much was expected of me. I was being entertained by the tribe of Oron and I just couldn't offend them in any way. I only hope my tale of the rat's meat didn't have too unsettling an effect on the ladies present at these meetings. I often jokingly used to tell them to look under their beds last thing at night to make sure there were no rats there and I've often wondered if they really did so.

At one church group meeting there was a highly emotional Indian gentleman in the audience who wanted to know why I was helping India.

"It's nothing to do with you. Let the rich of India help the poor," he raged. He was really excitable, blaming the British for the caste system and saying Britain should never have been in India. It began to get a bit ugly when he began ranting about the "Back to Basics" speech made by John Major, who was still Prime Minister at the time. I had to tell him to calm down and that I wasn't there to talk politics. All those there seemed to find the whole episode quite amusing. Afterwards he came up to me and bought one of my books. As he had been slightly critical of me I, naturally, was quite wary of him. If he wanted an argument, I was ready for him. As I always sign every book I sell, I ask people their names. When this particular gentleman came forward I fully expected him to be called Mohammad Venkataraghavan, or something similarly difficult to spell. But then he told me, in quite a loud voice: "My name's

Percy." He really did seem quite proud of his name and was smiling broadly. This very irate Indian gentleman, even though he had criticised most things British, gloried in the very British name of Percy.

The hospitality I've received from the different groups of people I've spoken to has been truly wonderful. Wherever I've been, the welcome has been warm and generous. There are not many villages within a 30-mile radius of where I live where I have not given one of my presentations. I've often had to get the map out to find exactly where these villages are, mind you, and on cold frosty nights I have travelled 30 miles or more in my car sometimes to find only seven people waiting for me. But seven people are, to me, hopefully seven books sold. In some respects it's not unlike selling life assurance, which was my job until I retired. This work, persuading people to buy life assurance, was put to good use when it came to persuading people to buy my book. It used to feel good when I clinched the sale of a policy, but selling copies of *My Indian Journey* is even better. Every hall I walk into, I feel a tremendous drive within me to sell my books and the satisfaction I get from doing it is colossal. Yes, I've loved speaking about India wherever I've been, and every penny I've taken from donations and book sales has gone to that school in India.

In the introduction to this book I've tried to explain why I've got so involved in helping India. It wasn't simply that I saw degradation and squalor that leaves a Westerner struggling for words to describe it. It was also because I had enormous feelings of guilt. The guilt I felt was very real indeed. My conscience would not let go of me because of what I'd seen. The starving millions, and in particular the people I'd seen in the streets with my own eyes, came to haunt me. Why had I been born in England and not India was a question that I repeatedly asked myself. Why had I been born so lucky? When I returned home from India in November 1991 with this overwhelming desire to help the country, I couldn't concentrate on anything else. Picking up an ordinary family life again was extremely difficult and getting involved in my work again was particularly hard. After three weeks in the subcontinent, keeping my mind on my insurance job was very taxing. I just couldn't forget India. I even felt guilty sometimes about being alive, such was the affect the country had on me. I then began to have the strangest of feelings. It was as though the people I'd met at Tongo were still very much with me. I actually felt them all around me and I could seemingly go nowhere without them. The Ursuline sisters at Tongo, Albina Kujur and even Albina's family - they were everywhere. I'd be sitting in my car at 8.30 on a cold winter evening having just completed my evening's insurance work and I'd feel the presence of those people in the car with me. This may be hard to believe, but it was the most extraordinary feeling and to me it was very real.

It certainly wasn't easy for my wife Kathleen either. She had not accompanied me on that first visit and it must have been very difficult for her to understand the feelings I was getting. To her it seemed that I either couldn't or wouldn't let India go. I'd come in from work, watch TV and within minutes I'd drift off into my own dream world of India. My wife would say: "You're thinking of India again, aren't you?" I just couldn't seem to shake off what I'd seen. It was as if I wasn't being allowed to. If the good Lord was trying to make me feel guilty, it was certainly working. Even now, as I write, the guilt has not left me.

The success, or should I say mini-success, of the *My Indian Journey* book has been a real bonus. When I'd written it I sent the manuscript to various publishers with high hopes of it being accepted. But alas none of them was sufficiently interested to publish it. I shouldn't have been too surprised because I know thousands of manuscripts are being submitted to publishers every year and only very few are accepted, but I was still disappointed. I knew I couldn't be a Jeffrey Archer, but even he had to start somewhere. Surely, after taking a year to write my book, I wasn't going to be denied a publisher. But this was the predicament I found myself in. I could have sent my manuscript to other publishers or waited a few years for one of them to accept it, but I couldn't afford to wait. It was absolutely imperative that repairs to the wall were started at the earliest possible opportunity. Waiting a few years for a publisher to accept my manuscript was not feasible. I had to act and the only way was to become a self-publisher, to put the book out myself. It was the only option left open to me.

I knew that becoming a self-publisher wasn't going to be straightforward. If I had been fortunate enough to find a publisher, they would have taken on the printing, marketing, promotion and selling of the book. Most importantly, the publisher would have made sure the book had been in all the bookshops up and down the country. I quickly realised that by going it alone I couldn't possibly distribute the book around the country myself, so I had to settle for my book being sold in the local bookshops. I had a good start because I was lucky enough to find a reputable printer who produced an attractive-looking book. Most importantly, the price was right. That was an important consideration, as I was bearing all the expense of publishing the manuscript. Fortunately, I recuperated my own money in no time once the book started to sell. It was a particularly worrying time because I could have lost a considerable amount of my money. It was quite a gamble, but to my absolute delight the book immediately began to sell. Just three months from the publication date in May 1993, I'd sold 500 books. Every so often I've been ordering additional books from my printer and so far I've sold nearly

3,000 copies. That's why I call it a mini-success. I hadn't a clue whether the book would sell or not. I know the sale of over 3,000 books wouldn't seem much to the Jilly Coopers of this world, but to me it meant that I could help that school in the wilds of the Indian countryside, and I couldn't have been more pleased.

Before I move on to *India Revisited* proper, I feel that, as *My Indian Journey* was written in order to rebuild that wall, it is only right and proper that I should mention the generosity of the people who bought my book, because without the money from those sales the wall might never have been repaired. The book has, somehow, found its way to many countries of the world, and the complimentary letters I've received have frequently been accompanied by a cheque and a note usually bearing a simple message along the lines of "get that wall repaired." It never ceased to surprise me that people, through reading my book, should send me a cheque. It amazed me that people should respond in such a way. I'd actually touched a nerve somewhere. Could I really have affected people in such a way? A secretary of an MP in Ottawa, Canada, sent a cheque for £30 and said she would be sponsoring a child in the Third World herself after reading my book. A Frenchman had bought the book in a secondhand bookshop in London. His hobby was collecting books on India and mine brought his total to 347. He sent me a cheque for £25 and also gave my wife and I a very cordial invitation to stay with him and his family in Paris. An elderly lady from Glasgow, who was well into her 80s, wrote: "I've been very lucky all my life but I realise, after reading your book, that others are not so lucky." She enclosed a cheque for £50. Nearer home, a Stamford man told me he had qualified for a tax relief of £43, but that he had decided to pass it on to me. "I shall not need this money because I've never had it," he wrote.

A deaconess also from Stamford on reading my book told me she couldn't put the wretched thing down. "Why wretched?" I asked.

"Because it took over my life. I was reading it at the breakfast table and the dinner table and any spare moment I could get," she told me.

A lady from Holbeach has since told me that after she heard me speak she bought my book and started reading it when she got home that evening. "I couldn't stop. My husband went to bed at 11.30pm leaving me reading your book. At 12.30 I joined him and sitting up beside him while he slept, I managed to finish it at 4.30am."

A friend of mine from Spalding took my book on holiday to Spain. On reading the book beside the swimming pool at his hotel he had tears in his eyes. "Never has a book affected me in such a way before," he told me. His wife told me that she had never seen him like that before. "Could I really have affected people in such a way?" I ask again.

Of all the letters received about the *My Indian Journey* book, there is one which I think stands out and portrays brilliantly the feelings of its writer. This letter, from a man who lives in Chester and works as an electrical engineer, probably touched me more than any other. He has given me permission to publish his letter. As I've said previously, I had no idea whether or not my book would be successful and sell. I was literally straying into unknown territory. Equally, we can never quite tell how others see us and, in my case, how others would feel about reading my book. To me, this man's word got to the heart of my Indian experience. If my book touched a nerve with readers, then I'm pleased. This well-written letter demonstrates how I touched a nerve with just one such reader.

Dear Brian,

Thank you for the copy of your book 'My Indian

Journey', which I have now read for the first time. I am not certain that I am able to pass any coherent opinions on it as yet, but will try to capture my first impressions now and then to give you a more objective view after a second reading.

Initially I was most interested in the profound effects the experience of being in India - and not the India of popular conception - seemed to be having on you. I had you taped as being the phlegmatic, stiff upper lip sort of man, you see. As I continued to read my perception began to change and I came to realise that your experiences were real, rather like climbing a mountain as opposed to just looking at it and imagining.

We in the West accept the deprivations and sufferings of others in total ignorance and with total equanimity until our eyes are opened by someone personally known to us. I had not realised that before and, while Albina Kujur's problems and difficulties distress me, your experiences startled me and I am no longer surprised at your need to write about them.

The community spirit you kept finding, the pride, the total faith and belief of the sisters and the commitment to the achievement of her goal by Albina suggest what it must have been like in our own rural areas until the First World War started to change it and materialism took over. It also suggests that the attitudes which we feel as liberal, or even liberated, people are somewhat callow and rather unrealistic. Perhaps our small towns and villages here in England (since we English seem to be blamed for nearly everyone else's problems) ought to be encouraged to twin themselves with villages in rural India and other such places in preference to towns and villages on the continent.

My PhD student, born here but from Gujarat via Uganda, is a very pleasant and helpful young man. He has also visited his relatives in India and gives the impression that he is amused by the acceptance of their difficult lives. Like me, he had not realised that those people do not really have much other choice. Having read your book for himself, he was first of all annoyed that you had even written such a book. Then, when he had finished it, he discovered that he was ashamed not to have seen what you saw for himself.

I cannot promise to give you anything more or better after my next reading of the book, but I will try to be more objective about its content. If nothing else you have made me at least look at the whole question of the existence of a vast number of fellow beings through different eyes.

When the wall was finally rebuilt about two years ago I knew in my bones I'd got to see it. It would provide the ideal focal point for the second visit to India that I had such a burning desire to make. The Ursuline sisters had always kept me informed about the wall in their regular letters to me. In all, it took about three years to rebuild. Work could only be done as and when I sent the sisters a cheque, so there was quite a lot of stopping and starting. When the wall was completed I continued sending money to the school and a new block of six classrooms was added to the existing building. In truth, I wanted to see for myself how the money I'd sent had been used. I knew I could trust my dear friends the Ursuline sisters at Tongo, but I had to see that the money had been put to its intended purpose. Also, I felt a duty to return to Tongo and report back to all those marvellous people who had supported my Indian project by buying my book, hearing me speak and sponsoring me on my London Marathon walk. People have often stopped me in the street to ask about the wall and whether it was built yet, and they had every right to know.

My second visit to India was not unlike the first

because not only did I again visit those places I'd been to before, but it was also tremendously exciting. I had never thought I could enjoy India as much as I had before, but I did. I described those first 22 days in my book as exhilarating and stimulating. However much I looked forward to the second visit, I thought, it couldn't possibly be anywhere near as good as before. But it was pulsating from start to finish. Just a few hours after leaving England, I landed in Calcutta as it was experiencing a cyclone. During the last half hour before landing, the aircraft seemed to hit some really stormy weather. It was a very bumpy ride, which left this passenger feeling extremely fidgety and nervous. Could this really be the India I'd dreamt of returning to during those last five years? Within hours of landing in Calcutta I began to wonder what I was doing in such an awful place.

My flight had got off to the worst possible start. As you will discover, the plane from Heathrow was 18 hours late because of technical difficulties - and that was to be just the start of a string of problems with all four of the flights I took. Once I finally got to Calcutta, I was again in a city that is so overcrowded that it claims to have one of the world's biggest slum areas. The poverty of the poor has to be seen to be believed, as scores die of malnutrition. I was to visit one slum area where one might think the inhabitants lived in some sort of hell, but I discovered that it was not hell at all. Despite all the degradation, I found a happiness there that was quite unbelievable. Also while in Calcutta I was once again to meet a living saint, Mother Teresa. Her health had deteriorated considerably since I had met her five years previously and it was a great loss to the world, and particularly the poor of Calcutta, when she died in September 1997, just 11 months after I met her that second time. Calcutta is a place full of British heritage and a colonial past readily symbolised by the old Victorian mansions and palaces spread throughout the city. The ghost of the British Raj lingers wherever one goes. Calcutta is a city of the dreadful night and the Black Hole, but it is also a city of great friendliness. The Bengali Indians from this part of north-east India are among the most friendly in the whole country. All this and much more adds up to making Calcutta a bewildering and bewitching city with an indomitable spirit.

In this book you will read of my reaction on seeing the completed school wall and of how, once back at the school, I received the shock of my life from the Ursuline sisters when they told me they were on strike. It's not possible, I thought. Not nuns, surely. My second spell in India was filled with many other highlights. At the Tongo school, there are some of the most beautifully behaved children to be found anywhere. Their singing reminded me that I was very much back in the world of The Sound of Music. One particular day I was taken to an area in South Bihar where it was hoped I might raise enough money to build a hospital to serve 700,000 people. On another occasion, I spent a day with Albina and her family and thought I was in the very heart of India. While at Tongo I also wanted to know if baby girls were murdered at birth. It was a practice I'd read about in England and apparently these horrendous acts are committed in certain areas of Bihar. I'm pleased to report, though, that female infanticide is not practised in Tongo. At Lohardaga I met an Ursuline sister who had made a miraculous recovery from cancer after attending a religious retreat where hundreds of sick people were in prayer. Because of her great faith in God she described her recovery as a miracle. Please believe me when I say miracles are being performed at these retreats all over India. You will read of my ten-hour journey through the night, the carriages packed to the rafters with people. It was sheer pandemonium at Ranchi railway station as people clamoured to get on that train. In the chapter aptly named 'A Train Passage to Calcutta' you will read also of my quite dramatic farewell to my friends at that station. Finally, you will hear of my fears for a young Indian girl who, because of circumstances beyond her control, could be faced with being drawn into prostitution.

I've tried once again to write from the heart with sincerity and honesty and I sincerely hope the book does not offend anyone or shock them excessively. There are also plenty of humorous incidents along the way, such as the occasion when I discussed with the Ursuline sisters what action I wanted to take against the chief government minister of Bihar, who had a broken leg. And of course there was the continuing trouble I had with my back. I really was in great pain, until one sister sent from heaven answered all my prayers. As regards offending anyone the last people I would want to offend would be the Ursuline sisters. I know when my previous book was published it was imperative that I should know the feelings of the sisters. Would they be hurt or sensitive to some of the things I'd written about them? After all they were Catholic nuns. But on receiving the book Sister Bernadette Tete wrote quickly back, saying how much she had enjoyed it. What was particularly pleasing to me, was when she also wrote that everything I'd written about India was true. Her letter was believe you me a relief. When this new book is published I shan't rest until I hear the sisters' reaction to it, I'd sooner have not written the book if I was to hurt them in any way.

The reason for this second book on India is to continue to help the school. I know of no other way of raising the money. If I did I would try it. Hopefully this sequel to *My Indian Journey* will do just that. You see, I do have a dream, a sort of vision for the future of the whole area of Tongo, a Golden Vision in which even more Indian children can attend that school out in the wilds of the subcontinent of India. I shall explain 'The Golden Vision' in more detail at the end of this book. It is something beautiful which affects the innocents of Tongo. Only from the sale of *India Revisited* can I continue to help them.

So, Mr Brian, as I was forever being called during my travels in India, had once again packed his suitcase and was bound for the land of fantasy, dreams, colour and intrigue once more. My flight would take me from Heathrow Airport to that metropolis of throbbing vitality and teeming millions known as Calcutta. The adrenaline was pumping so much that I was very nearly bursting. Yet, surprisingly, I was also getting nervous. India had exactly the same effect shortly before my first visit. The reason for this is that while in India I had the feeling that literally anything could happen at any time. But I really was ready for another great adventure. Here was I, a grandfather three times over, acting like an excitable schoolboy once again. I really should control my emotions more, I kept thinking. And, like a bright dazzling star in the east, India beckoned, and it was drawing me to it like a magnet.

Chapter One

Heathrow Heartbreak

The British Airways aircraft finally roared down the runway at Heathrow Airport, bound for New Delhi, India, over eighteen hours late. The flight should have taken off on the evening of October 26, 1996, at 9.55pm, but because of technical difficulties the plane was grounded for many hours.

The day had started well enough. Up at 6am to prepare for my flight to India, I'd said goodbye to my wife at my daughter's home and I was driven from my home by my son and son-in-law to Heathrow. On finding Terminal Four I said my goodbyes to them, too, and settled down in the lounge ready for the evening flight. What excitement I'd felt as I sat in the hustle and bustle of that airport lounge. Was I really going back to India? I wouldn't really believe it until I was actually on the plane. It had always been my ambition to return to India, and I was going for two weeks. All these thoughts were going through my mind sitting in that lounge. Could this second trip be as good as the first time? But I'd desperately needed to go back. And I wanted once again to meet some very special friends.

Then, over the Tannoy came the news that Flight 143 was cancelled, and it wouldn't be taking off until well into the next day. I was shattered - one minute all keyed up and raring to go, the next emptiness and going nowhere. But my disappointment was clearly nothing compared to that of some very angry passengers on the same flight, mostly Indians I might add, who just wouldn't accept that the flight was cancelled. Because of that they got very aggressive indeed. The main reason they'd got so restless was that after we'd been told the flight had been cancelled until the following afternoon there was no further information. People started muttering amongst themselves about where they would be spending the night. After many hours hanging around the Terminal Four lounge we knew absolutely nothing, with no information coming through at all. This caused some very agitated Indians to gather round the reception desk demanding to know more. They even started thumping their clenched fists on the desk. The two lady assistants couldn't cope. People were shouting and losing their tempers. It looked as if things were getting out of control and the police were called. I couldn't help but feel sorry for those two ladies.They didn't deserve the criticism they were getting. But what I failed to understand was the reason for this lack of information. Surely passengers whose flight has been cancelled have every right to know what's going on. Surely Heathrow Airport should be ready for any emergency that comes along. What a way to start my return visit to India. Like a lot of those passengers, I was becoming increasingly disillusioned.

Just before midnight we were told there was a coach outside the terminal waiting to take us to Birmingham for the night. We had been told that not one hotel in the whole of the London area could put more than 300 passengers up for the night. Well, I wasn't going to Birmingham. Goodness knows what time I would get to bed there. I had decided to sleep on the floor of the lounge we were in, however uncomfortable it was going to be. It was then that Ron and Joan Luff, to whom I will be forever grateful, came to my rescue. I had got talking to this couple at the reception desk and when we were told we were going to Birmingham they told me that as they lived in Twickenham, which was only a few miles from Heathrow, they would be going home for the night. They asked me if I'd like to go with them, as they had a spare bed. I instantly took them up on their most generous offer. I therefore had a good night's sleep and breakfast, making my way back to Heathrow with them for the afternoon flight to New Delhi. This couple didn't know me from Adam, they hadn't a clue who I was, yet they were prepared to take a complete stranger into their home for the night. It was indeed my good fortune to have met them.

Flight 143 finally left Heathrow at 5.35pm on October 27. Even then it was behind the new scheduled time we had been given. It was supposed to have taken off at 3.30pm, so we were really over 18 hours late.

I settled down for a long flight of seven hours to New Delhi, where the Twickenham couple would be disembarking. They were going on a package tour of north east India. I would be staying on the aircraft, which would then be flying on to Calcutta. On that plane I thought of my wife Kathleen. I wanted so much for her to come with me, but her doctor had advised her she would be wise not to go to India. We had to heed that advice. I had been in Ranchi Hospital when last in India. I dreaded to think about the state my wife would have been in if she'd wound up there. I had the feeling myself that if I'd fallen ill and been taken there I'd have been lucky to come out alive. I can still remember how filthy it was. I couldn't believe what I was seeing. We should never grumble about the health service in Britain - in fact, we should praise it. In England we take so many things for granted, including a marvellous health service.

Also on that plane I thought about Albina Kujur, the girl I'd sponsored from the age of 11 through the charity ActionAid. A year ago I'd received her letter, telling me she'd passed her exams. She was a schoolteacher at last. What a thrill it was going to be for me to meet her again. I also thought of the Ursuline Sisters of Bihar, my very special friends who I'd affectionately named The Divine

Sisters of Tongo when I met them previously. I thought of the school wall and classrooms being built. I couldn't wait to get to Tongo, that idyllic spot I'd found in deepest Bihar.

When I last visited India I was still working, but four years ago I was made redundant through early retirement. I consider myself quite fortunate to have kept working to the age of 58, but after twenty-nine-and-a-half years as the Man from the Pru I was leaving. The Prudential had been a great company to work for and I'm extremely proud to have done just that. I actually enjoyed my work, but like all jobs mine had changed. The last three years had seen considerable changes, and the older one gets the more one resents change - me included. Exams had to be passed in order to sell life assurance. This I'd found particularly hard and it worried me constantly. I felt I was back at school. I'd sold life assurance for all those years and I was being told that in order to get a certificate I had to pass the necessary exams. If I couldn't pass, there would be no certificate. My job was threatened. Yes, the Pru had changed and now it's a young man's game. Redundancy came at just the right time for me. The company finished more than 1,000 of its employees, but it had given me an excellent pension and for that I will be most grateful. I've always said that if my body were ever opened up, the name Prudential would be in there. That's how much I've enjoyed working for the company. I really was proud to have been known as the Man from the Pru.

When one sits on a plane, all sorts of things cross one's mind. I thought of cricket. Last time I visited India I was still playing the game. My intention was to play to the age of 60, but a swollen ankle put a stop to that. The strange thing is that I can do marathon walks, but I can't run, and if one can't run, one can't play cricket. I actually retired from regular cricket at 58, so I'm thankful for such a long innings. I've played most sports, but nothing compares to cricket. I'm still involved at grass-roots level. If the Prudential is in my blood, then cricket is definitely there, too.

Sitting on that plane I remembered the time, only a year before, when my wife and I, our daughter and her husband and three grandchildren were in an aircraft that had to make an emergency landing at Luton Airport. The plane had developed engine trouble and halfway to Menorca we turned back. The captain kept assuring the passengers there was nothing to worry about. Can you imagine how we felt, with me a notoriously bad flyer, when over the Tannoy the captain said as we approached Luton Airport: "This is the captain speaking. Do not be alarmed, but we are going to make an emergency landing. All traffic in the area has been stopped and roads around the airport have been cut off. The airport is waiting for us on full emergency alert, so do not be alarmed if, as we touch down, you see fire engines rushing out to greet us." Everyone looked at each other. This is it, I thought. Suddenly, all the babies and children who had been getting increasingly restless after such a long flight, became very quiet. All noise had stopped, not one baby was crying. The plane was packed with holidaymakers and dozens of children were on board. As that plane gently eased its way down from the clouds above Luton Airport, I'm sure many prayers were being said. There was the most deathly silence imaginable. It really was uncanny. I managed to look out of one of the windows and, sure enough, as the plane touched down the fire engines were rushing out to greet us in the event of fire breaking out as we hit the runway. All at once, those passengers knew they'd make it. The plane made a perfect landing and spontaneous clapping and cheering broke out, more through relief than anything else, I think. And here was I sitting on this plane to India once again thinking about air crashes. I know that as long as I live I shall never be entirely comfortable in an aircraft but I also know that to visit faraway places in the world, air travel is by far the best way.

Something that has always intrigued me while sitting on an aircraft is how an atheist copes with death, particularly when they are involved in an emergency situation like this. Although I am a self-confessed bad flyer, I do at least have my faith, but an atheist is a non-believer, so what would their feelings be as the plane neared Luton Airport? As I've already said, I was sure many prayers were being said as that aircraft gently eased its way out of the clouds for its final approach and I don't mind admitting that I was saying mine. But what of a person who has rejected God completely and who has no faith whatsoever? Everyone has the right to be a non-believer if they so wish, but how do they cope in a situation where they are likely to be facing death? Would they be saying "well, this is it, this is the end of my life, goodbye all," because the real atheist, who is sincere in his non-belief, would definitely not be saying his prayers. Atheists have actually said to me about religion "I don't believe in all that rubbish." What would an atheist be thinking if they were on a plane nose-diving out of control towards the ground? What would those split-second thoughts be as they knew the end was near, as they faced the final curtain? You see, I believe an atheist might possibly be saying to themselves as they approach their death "I know I've never believed in God, but if there is a God please save me. I don't want to die." As they face death they might well believe that there is a God after all and they might appeal to someone. No one wants to die in a plane crash, least of all me, and I know my prayers were giving me some comfort on that plane as it prepared to touch down. But what has the non-believer got? They must surely feel so alone. I know what situation I'd sooner be in. I'd rather have my faith, which never leaves me, because there are certain times in this world when we really need it.

As I sat on that plane coming into Dum Dum Airport, Calcutta, terrible thoughts, like plane crashes, were again coming into my head. It was literally pouring with rain and the plane seemed to be battling against gale-force winds. On looking through the side window, all I could see was thick fog. For a few dreadful minutes I feared the worst. It was a really bumpy ride, believe me. Would the captain be able to see where he was going, I asked myself stupidly. I was in God's hands entirely, but I need not have worried - the landing was as perfect as any could be. Having altered my watch to Indian time, it was midday. What relief I felt. That star in the east had directed me safely to India once again. As I came off that plane and down the steps I was tingling with excitement. I was on Indian soil once more, but what a welcome the weather gave me. It was raining hard, with strong, gusty winds. I hadn't met weather like this when I was here before. It really was the most miserable day it could possibly have been.

Chapter Two

Feelings

There's a cricketer's wife at Market Deeping Cricket Club who has said to me on numerous occasions: "How's your feelings, Brian?" I usually reply by informing her that my feelings, of whatever nature, are functioning very nicely, thank you. Many years ago she saw me in a very tight clinch situation with my wife, dancing to the ballad 'Feelings', which is of course quite a romantic song to dance to. Even now when I see her she enquires about my feelings. Whether she thinks that because of the advancing years my feelings should lessen, I'm not quite sure, but I have feelings just like anyone else and my feelings on seeing Calcutta again were of an entirely different nature to what was happening on that dance floor. The words for the song 'Feelings' say that tear drops are falling down my face. Well tear drops were not shed, just depression, loads of depression, because it was an highly emotional experience for me to be in that city again. My feelings were of such shock that, to quote a cricketing expression, I was hit for six. I thought I could handle what I was about to see, but I couldn't. It left me numb. Never in my whole life have I been so shaken by what I saw. This was the effect this over-populated city was to have on me. I was once again in the Calcutta of Job Charnock, the Englishman who founded the place in 1687 on the banks of the river Houghly. The population of the city is now estimated at 13 million. Seeing it again reminded me of the book *The City of Joy*. It was written by Frenchman Dominique Lapierre and became an international number one bestseller. He describes Calcutta as a hell of a town, perhaps the most terrible place in the world. In order to tell his epic story he actually lived in one of the slum areas of the city for many months. On reading his book, I was rivetted by it. He found the very heart of the city and, to my surprise, I did too.

On arriving in Calcutta I found that a cyclone had hit many parts of north east India, and East Bengal in particular. No wonder that aircraft I'd travelled on had met such stormy weather as it approached the airport. The coastal areas around Calcutta had been severely damaged. Little villages had been swept away, hundreds of people having lost their lives. There was flooding on a massive scale. Calcutta seemed to have caught the edge of it, with no damage done, but it had evidently been raining for days. These were not the usual monsoon rains, which come once a year, but something different. In this part of the world, cyclones are an ever-increasing threat. Nearly every year, India's neighbour to the east, Bangladesh, has dreadful flooding and sometimes thousands die. I could only hope the rains would stop. Calcutta in the rain must be one of the grimmest sights on earth and on this second visit I was seeing it at its worst, and it was a depressing experience. Last time I was in the city the sun shone every day. Even Calcutta can look quite good in parts when the sun comes out, but it was pouring with rain. My feelings would hardly describe the place as The City of Joy - quite the reverse, I can assure you.

The aircraft had touched down at Dum Dum Airport at midday. Considering it had taken off 18 hours late from Heathrow, it had made up for lost time considerably. At the airport I was to experience the usual hassle that any traveller experiences as he comes out of the main entrance building. I was confronted by the usual beggars. They made a beeline for me. I was white and had money, or so they thought. A young mother with her baby in her arms pleaded with me to give her some rupees. "Please,

please," she kept saying, please being of course the only word of English she could speak. In no time I was swamped by these poor people. I could hardly move. It was at this point that a young man shouted "Taxi, sir!" and in no time my suitcase and hand luggage were whisked away with me in hot pursuit of a waiting taxi. Even in the taxi they wouldn't leave me alone. It was surrounded by beggars, hands coming in all directions through the windows. I then gave the young mother some rupees and with that the pleading intensified. Children scratching at the windows with fear in their eyes wouldn't leave me alone. The taxi driver put his foot down and we moved off at speed and I knew as I sat in the car that I was well and truly in Calcutta again.

The taxi ride from the airport to the hotel can be quite a culture shock. Having done it before, I was surprised that it still shocked me the way it did. I was filled with despondency at the sheer hopelessness of the situation and what I saw through the taxi window filled me with despair. It is worth repeating that Calcutta in the rain is a sight one can never forget. The thousands of skinny, undernourished people walking miserably in the rain as if in a dream, the children - certainly none of them laughing - looking sad and pitiful, the dogs never wagging their tails, and the sacred cows strolling oh so slowly amidst the filth and squalor of this run-down city. All this I saw as the rain fell in bucket-fulls. I really did feel depressed about what I was seeing. The city shocked me far more than before.

The taxi ride was precarious to say the least, which didn't help the day, either. The young man who had said "Taxi, sir!" was not the taxi driver. He sat in the front passenger seat with me in the back. I'd told him I wanted the Kenilworth Hotel in Russel Street, the hotel I'd stayed at when last in the city. He then proceeded to tell me he could get me a hotel much cheaper than the Kenilworth but just as good. I told him I wasn't interested, but he went on and on. Finally, he could see I wasn't interested in this hotel and at the traffic lights right in the middle of the city he simply opened his passenger door and disappeared into the crowded streets. I asked the driver where he'd gone and quickly realised he couldn't speak a word of English. I also sensed I could be in a very awkward situation. Here I was, barely an hour in a foreign country in a city of millions, with it raining cats and dogs and accompanied by a driver I couldn't communicate with at all. I began to feel vulnerable. He hadn't any idea what I was saying. I kept shouting "Kenilworth Hotel, Russel Street," but he was totally oblivious to what I was saying. I suppose I could have opened the door and run, but my suitcases were in the boot. So, I couldn't leave. I was in the driver's pocket and with kidnapping on the increase I was well aware of the situation. Then another taxi driver nearly hit our taxi and I witnessed road rage Indian style. My driver went completely bonkers, racing after the other taxi with his horn blaring and dodging in and out of the very busy traffic as if on the fairground dodgems. He caught up with the offending taxi at traffic lights and gave the driver a mouthful of abuse. Eventually he calmed down and I had began to recognise various parts of the city again, so with my directions we reached Russel Street and the Kenilworth Hotel. I was only too thankful that we had made it and that I was never going to be seeing that taxi driver again.

On checking into the hotel I made my way to my room. I felt really low. I opened my suitcase and it was just as my wife had packed it. All at once I missed her dreadfully and I felt so lonely. What I'd seen on the streets had depressed me far more than I'm able to say. I began to question what I was doing there. How could I leave my wife and family and come to such a dreadful place? I would have given anything to be back home in Market Deeping. What I couldn't understand was that I'd enjoyed my stay so much the last time I'd been in that city. There was unbelievable squalor then, so why was it affecting me so differently this second time? I thought of my wife's words. She had said: "Go and see India again. Get it out of your system once and for all and when you're ready, return home to us." I've called this chapter Feelings. My feelings on that first day concerned the people of Calcutta. How do people survive in this place? Those poor miserable souls. Their feelings must be of gloom and despondency. Perhaps they don't have feelings in that sense and perhaps that's the secret of getting through each day.

That evening I went into the hotel lounge. I just had to get out of my room. I just wanted to talk to someone and in the lounge I quickly got talking to two Indian businessmen. It's surprisingly easy to form conversations with people who go out of their way to welcome you. These two men were both in their early 30s. After exchanging pleasantries, mostly about the weather for some reason, we got talking about marriage, Indian style. I said marriages were breaking down more and more in England and I asked these businessmen if they thought arranged marriages worked. I couldn't have picked two better examples of Indian marriages. They each had a child. Businessman no. 1 informed me that his was an arranged marriage. He had only met his wife once before the wedding. The marriage was arranged by both sets of parents. He admitted that on the wedding day he didn't love his wife, but said that after three years of marriage he did now love her. He also told me what wise parents he had and that he would be eternally grateful to them for his arranged marriage. "I trusted my parents implicitly to find the right girl for me," he said. He added how important it was that his wife was a virgin on their wedding day and said he could not have married a girl who played around. "If I'd found that my wife had deceived me, we would have separated," he said, "but I need not have worried. My parents knew exactly what was required."

Businessman no. 2 told me he married his wife for love. "I fell madly in love with her," he said. "I still love my wife, but she is difficult and unreasonable. She is a village girl from Orissa. She never wanted to leave that village." On marrying his wife, he took her to live with his parents in Calcutta, but she couldn't get on with them. "When my son was born, she took him home to her village and stayed there. I now hardly see my son at all, but she won't listen to reason. My son, my son - oh, how I miss him," he said.

After spending two hours with my new-found Hindu friends I retired to my room. I had plenty of food for thought. Two marriages, one Indian-style and working well, the other one more traditional to the Western eye but floundering. Businessman no. 1 had fully expected his wife to be a virgin on their wedding day and was now devoted to her. He respected her so much for saving herself for him. How many brides are there in England these days who save themselves in such a way?

That conversation with those two Indian businessmen, incidentally, reminds me of when, just a day later I'd got talking to one of the Indian girl receptionists in the hotel. She was about 25 years of age and having got to know her slightly, I wanted to know more about her. I was most interested in these arranged marriages and I wanted to know if this girl was married, and if not, why not? Marriages being arranged by parents, intrigued me and I wanted to know more. She could have told me to mind my own business but she didn't. In fact she seemed quite prepared to talk. She told me she was single. "My parents know exactly what I want and I trust them completely in finding the right marriage partner for me," she said, and with typical Indian frankness and speaking very good English she continued. "I've never been with a man before, because I'm saving myself for that very special person and I know that when I marry, whoever that might be, I shall be very happy and I shall love him forever," she said.

At the breakfast table next morning I got talking to an Indian lady who, I discovered after introducing myself, lived in America. She and her Indian husband had lived in Los Angeles for 17 years. Previously she had lived in Kent. "I liked England, but where I am now, in LA, it's on the coast and it's all so beautiful. I am so happy there," she said. But she also said how guilty she felt on returning to India. She was born in Calcutta and spent her early life there.

"Those poor people out on the streets have nothing and I've got everything. How lucky I've been, but right now I feel so guilty," she repeated. I could only agree with her, saying how lucky I was to have been born in England. "Yes, we are both lucky. Once I'm back in America I shall forget about this place, but seeing poverty such as there is here distresses me." With that, she got up, saying: "Goodbye, Mr Brian, and have a good holiday." We shook hands. It's strange how people come into one's life for half an hour or so and pour out feelings about being Calcutta and then disappear, never to be seen again. She was a highly intelligent lady, who spoke perfect English. As my flight to Ranchi was that afternoon and hers to America was at midnight, I was sure she was one person who I would never set eyes on again.

My world was shattered an hour later at the reception desk. I'd asked the staff to confirm my flight to Ranchi at 3.20pm, but a few minutes later the assistant manager informed me very apologetically that my flight had taken off at 9am. It had been brought forward six hours with nobody at the airport bothering to tell me. I was livid. I'd heard of flights being put back six hours, but never forward. My plans were in turmoil. I immediately thought of the Ursuline sisters and Albina, who would be waiting for me at Ranchi Airport. I managed to telephone the convent school at Ranchi to pass on the message that I wouldn't be coming that day. My new flight was two days later on the Thursday. At least I'd got a message through. I knew they'd be just as disappointed as I was, though I was indeed very lucky that the telephone was working because many lines had been blown down by the cyclone. But I felt so despondent. Through no fault of my own I'd let down some very special people. Also, what was I going to do in this city for an extra two days? I'd promised my family that I wouldn't go out alone in the city, but I couldn't just stay in the hotel for two days. I'd got to get out. It was then that I thought of Mother Teresa, the world-famous Christian lady known as The Angel of Calcutta. I'd met her five years ago. Why not go to her orphanage and inquire how she was? They might even let me see her, I thought, while wondering at the same time if I could really be that lucky again.

Mother Teresa had been quite seriously ill for some time. Over the previous two years she had had at least three heart attacks to my knowledge. Also, she had fallen and broken her collarbone. In the last 12 months she had been in and out of hospital with heart and chest problems. In addition, she was suffering from malaria - so there was certainly no shortage of health problems for her to contend with. I knew from reading English newspapers before arriving in Calcutta that she was quite ill. Having met her before, I took a particular interest in news about her. I couldn't forget her.

This great Christian lady was born on August 26, 1910, in Skorje, Macedonia, which was then part of the kingdom of Albania. Albania was at that time, as it is now, one of the poorest countries in the world, although Mother Teresa didn't necessarily have a poor upbringing because her father, a builder, was able to give the family a reasonable standard of living. Brought up in the Catholic religion, it was at the age of 12 that she first felt the desire to become a nun. At the age of 18 she arrived in Ireland and joined the sisters of Loreto. During just a few months in Ireland she became quite fluent in English. In November of the same year, 1928, she arrived in Calcutta.

So, at the age of 19 she arrived in India, and soon afterwards, she took her vows of poverty, chastity and obedience. She had committed herself, from that point on, to God and to the poorest of the poor in Calcutta, where the impoverished masses died in shocking numbers, usually from malnutrition. Because of the effect on her of seeing human beings dying on the streets of the city, Mother Teresa opened the first of her Missionaries of Charity. It had taken her 20 years from the time she arrived in Calcutta. Her very first home was opened in the place where she felt the need was greatest, right in the slums, and the dying destitute somehow dragged their skeleton-like bodies to it. There they would be cared for by Mother Teresa and her co-workers. She and her fellow nuns all wore the distinctive white sari with the blue border which became her trade mark, so to speak. The lucky ones who made it to the home at least had love and comfort while they lay dying. The unlucky ones continued to die on the streets. Mother Teresa began opening other homes and orphanages, and now they are spread across 100 countries all over the world. In recognition of her work, she has been lavished with the highest honours, including probably the highest of them all, the Nobel Peace Prize, which she received in 1979. This, then, was the lady I wished to meet again, this saint of the slums, as she is known. I didn't give myself much chance of doing so, though. She could well have been in hospital and even if she was at her Missionaries of Charity, her Mother House, as she called it, she might be too ill to see anyone, but to my delight and surprise I was allowed to see her again. She had been discharged from hospital only the day before.

I hailed a taxi and I was taken through the usual squalor of the packed streets to her home for the destitute on the city's lower circular road. On arrival I was surprised not to see the usual knot of shockingly ill people outside. Five years before, there had seemed to be dozens of the dying and destitute literally lying on the pavement or scattered about the roadside and hoping to be admitted. I've since learnt that the Mother House is no longer a home and although people are still cared for there, they are present in nothing like the numbers they used to be. I was told when I arrived at 12.30pm that if I wished to see Mother Teresa I should return at 4pm and then, with a group of other people, I could perhaps meet her. So, at 4pm I presented myself again at the Mother House and was ushered by Mother Teresa's nuns, with a small group of about 20 American tourists, to wait near the chapel. The Mother House, is, I might add, just an ordinary three-storey Victorian building. It was just as I'd remembered it. It's so ordinary that, were it not for a board on the wall outside bearing the words Missionaries of Charity, one could quite easily pass by without noticing it. I began talking to an Ohio couple and the man asked me if I would take a photo with his camera of him with Mother Teresa, should we be lucky enough to see her. I then asked him to do the same for me. After about five minutes of chatting to these tourists, who should come through a side door in the chapel, being pushed in a wheelchair, but Mother Teresa. I could tell the Americans were really excited about seeing her. The look on their faces told me they couldn't quite believe it. We were told we would be given just a couple of minutes each to talk to her individually. On seeing her myself I realised immediately that this was not the same Mother Teresa I had met five years ago. That first meeting I had with her is still so very clear in my mind today and I'll just briefly recall my feelings about that particular occasion. I suppose I was in awe of Mother Teresa, but I need not have worried because this very frail little elderly lady put me completely at ease. At once I noticed an extraordinary atmosphere between us which I'd never felt with anyone else. It was as if there was an invisible spirit nearby. She took my hand and as we sat on a little bench outside the chapel she asked me why I was in India. She seemed most interested in Albina Kujur and my wish finally to meet her.

"You must be very proud of that girl," Mother Teresa said to me. For five magical minutes I spoke to this lady. She was taking such an interest in me, as if I was the only person that mattered to her at that particular moment. Anyone who has ever met her will mention this feeling of being made to feel important to her. She had put me so completely at ease that I felt I was in conversation with an old friend. I had to pinch myself, I couldn't believe I was in the company of a world-famous Christian person. I realised very quickly that her sense of humanity was very much part of her personality and her courteous and gracious manner made me feel such compassion for her. Conversation with her was so easy and natural. For those few minutes I was hers and she was mine. Her love and concern for me made me feel as though I wanted to put my arm around her. This really dear, sweet, 83-year-old lady who had mixed with presidents, prime ministers and royalty had me spellbound. This lady, who was the poor people's best friend, had the best possible values and her love of God and people filled me with such admiration for her that perhaps only those who have met her will know what I'm talking about. This lady had given so much love and comfort to millions of poor people throughout the world and her love was the same whether the person was Christian, Hindu, Muslim or Sikh.

At my talks and slide shows I always felt the highlight would be when I spoke to Mother Teresa of Calcutta. There was always no shortage of questions to answer.

But my second meeting with her was very different, as when I went to take her hand I could see she was very ill indeed. Her voice had always been soft but this time I couldn't really hear her at all. I remember inquiring about her health and mentioning that I'd met her five years ago. She nodded as if she knew that, but I doubt it. She looked extremely frail and weak and I knew she couldn't possibly live for long in that condition. But, even though she was so dreadfully ill, I still felt that presence I had felt before. She looked so small and helpless sitting in that wheelchair. I suppose I was saying goodbye to an old friend who had gone out of her way to make me feel so at ease with her. One of the greatest figures of the 20th century, admired and respected worldwide, was on the point of leaving this life. Nobody would be more prepared for death. In fact, she had always said she looked forward to it. Having said that, she had a great constitution and was a fighter every inch of the way, but I knew she couldn't possibly get better. I can only say that I believe, like many others, that the world will be a worse place without her. I know I've been lucky most of my life and I've been lucky to meet Mother Teresa twice. She's someone, who, I can assure you, I am unlikely to forget and I shall reflect on her passing in the last chapter of this book.

All over the city of Calcutta there is a lost empire. Behind those pavements that are so covered with people is ample evidence of colonial power and what Great Britain was to India. One doesn't have to look too far to find it. There are British-built mansions and minor palaces to be found everywhere. Often classical in design, they give a dramatic picture of what life was like under the rule of the Raj.

With the passing years, though, these Georgian-type villas are now in ruins. Literally falling down, they are. They must have been magnificent buildings in their heyday. Their tiers of columns give way to great architectural monuments built by British engineers. There must be hundreds of these superbly-built mansions in the city, but the years of neglect, rotting and decay have turned them into a rather depressing spectacle, a shadow of what once was. They are in a filthy condition and often occupied by squatters. I read only recently that a Calcutta government official had said these buildings, which are works of art, should be preserved purely because they are British and part of Indian heritage, and that history shouldn't be forgotten. At least someone in government appreciates the importance of these increasingly ruined buildings. How proud they must have been when they were built in the 19th century, or in some cases before. The reality, though, is that they will just fade away and finally be pulled down because the Calcutta government does not have the money to bring some of the finest Victorian architectural monuments built by the British back to their former glory. These palaces and mansions were built in a different age and nothing can prevent them from remaining there. They are an abiding reminder of the Raj of India. One can only imagine their wonderfully lavish and impressive grandeur and splendour, and seeing them now reduces one to extreme sadness. The British gave India its independence in 1947 and those great villas and palaces stand just as they were left, and they will continue to disintegrate.

In the hotel lounge that evening somebody patted me on the shoulder and said: "Hello, Mr Brian - what are you doing here? I thought your flight left this afternoon." It was the Indian lady who lived in America who I'd spoken to at the breakfast table that morning. We went and sat down and I told her what had happened. "This is outrageous.

Indian Airlines can't just bring a flight forward by six hours. Let's go and see the hotel manager. We will sue them," she said. The manager sent for the office girl who had telephoned the airport earlier and she told the Indian lady of the conversation. By now she had told me her name was Runu. "Let Indian Airways pay for their own competence. Claim all expenses including hotel bills and send the details off as quickly as possible when you get home," she said. I thanked her for the very businesslike way in which she had dealt with my problem, but in all honesty I was quite capable of working out what I would be claiming for when I got home.

Once back in the lounge with Runu, she wanted to know what I was doing in India. I told her that five years ago I had spent the most exhilarating 22 days of my life in India and that it had always been my ambition to return. I also told her that because of my experiences in India I had written a book, and, as I'd brought several copies of *My Indian Journey* with me, I went to my room to fetch one, signed it and gave it to her. I felt that in view of her having been so very helpful over my cancelled flight, it was the least I could do. It was my gift to her, I told her. She told me she was a book manager at St. Margaret's Episcopal School near her home in Los Angeles. Apparently there are more than 2,000 pupils at this school. When she had read my book, she said, it would be put in the school library so the whole school could read it. She seemed most interested in the book having been inspired by my sponsorship of an Indian girl, who I'd finally met. "Your book seems very educational to me and I shall really push orders for you," she said. I might add that my conversation with Runu in that lounge was held in the presence of an Indian man friend of hers. Her husband had been unable to make this particular trip, she told me. Her brother, who lives in Calcutta, then appeared in the lounge and I was introduced to him. He was, his sister told me, a highly successful businessman in the city. He looked to me to be from one of the high castes of Indian society, one of the rich Hindus, no doubt. But he was extremely pleasant and I couldn't have asked for a more courteous companion. He really went out of his way to make me feel comfortable in his presence. Time was marching on and Runu said her midnight flight home was drawing closer. As we shook hands she said: "Goodbye, Mr Brian. You will certainly be hearing from me again. I shall start to read your book on the plane." She seemed convinced she could sell my book in America. I was getting mildly excited about the prospect of it taking off there. If only it could, I remember thinking. Then, and only then, would I be able to make some real money for the Ursuline convent school in the village of Tongo in faraway southern Bihar.

Having arrived in Calcutta on the Monday I had until the Thursday to see as much of the place as I possibly could, and after recovering somewhat from the shock of seeing the city again in a torrential downpour I was slowly coming round to feeling the affection I had for it before. But, even so, I still felt something was missing and I couldn't put my finger on why. I suppose when one leaves a country such as England, obviously one of the foremost nations on Earth, and steps off an aircraft into a Calcutta recently hit by a cyclone one should be prepared for the biggest culture shock ever. This is what happened to me, but I wasn't prepared for it and I was shaken rigid. The city is synonymous with poverty and squalor and until there is a complete overhaul of the place this will remain so. Shanty towns are spread all over the city. Unbelievable poverty is the only phrase I can find to describe it. Yet amidst all its degradation it inspires a respect and affection in many who, like me, have seen it before. For one thing, its people are kind, imaginative, most hospitable and always prepared to talk. Some have a reasonable command of the English language, which undoubtedly helps with a person such as myself, who cannot speak the Indian languages. I don't think I've been so depressed in all my life as I was when I arrived at the beautiful Kenilworth Hotel on my first day in the city. After taking that taxi ride in an absolute downpour through such a tremendous concentration of traffic, where horn blowing reaches an all-time high, with a taxi driver who acted like a madman, and seeing the sheer squalor of Calcutta I felt utterly dejected and experienced great loneliness. What I had seen had left me numb, but having mentioned my loneliness I would add that Calcutta is just about the least lonely place on earth. One could never be lonely there for long. When I was last in the city I was overwhelmed by the friendliness of its people. Out on the streets I was forever talking to them. Could I again find the very soul of the city that I'd discovered before? I was searching for a certain something that I knew existed, but alas I hadn't found it. Maybe the weather didn't help, for although it had stopped raining from the Tuesday onwards it was very dull indeed - as though a cloud from the cyclone had settled over the city and wouldn't be shifted.

Every day Balaram, the taxi driver recommended to me by the hotel, would pick me up and take me round Calcutta. I went on many a tour of the city and although one thinks straight away of terrible slums and impoverished people, thousands of them living in little mud huts called bustees, there is also a different side to the city. Calcutta today is a city that retains many splendours of yesteryear. Its presence is near-regal, imposing and memorable. Englishman Job Charnock will forever be linked to the city. It sprang up from a cluster of villages and grew so rapidly that it was soon to become the British Empire's second-largest city, after London. The British of course took over responsibility for the whole country, not just Calcutta. Colonialism certainly played its part in India and because Britain was there for hundreds of years it left its mark, particularly in the towns and cities and nowhere more so than in Calcutta. The British presence is everywhere. Around every street corner it's there - Victorian buildings, the bumpy and filthy roads with street names, all of them British - one can even breathe and smell the atmosphere of being in a British city. One simply cannot escape the old country. One of the great buildings of the city is the Victorian Memorial Hall - so proudly it stands in its white marble in beautiful grounds and lakes. The Government buildings, the Writers' Building, St. Paul's Cathedral and British-built churches scattered all over the city make one feel proud to be British. British sports and pastimes are played in abundance, and among the great stadia are the Eden Gardens cricket ground, the soccer grounds and the racecourse. Golf, played at the Royal Golf Club, and hockey are both great British pastimes, or should I say institutions, which are widely enjoyed here.

How on earth could an Englishman feel lonely in Calcutta? The city also has a magnificent shopping area with shops every bit as good as the West End of London. Wouldn't my wife have loved to have gone shopping there. There are bargains galore. And lastly, having covered most things British, come the British cemeteries, where thousands of British soldiers lie and serve as a reminder of the price Great Britain paid for being in India.

While in Calcutta I was determined to meet the Pavement Doctor. Three years ago I'd read a book called *Doctor Jack*. I've done a lot of reading about India in the last five years and there were three books I'd found particularly absorbing. They were *The City of Joy, Mother Teresa* and *Doctor Jack*. Dr Jack Preger was born in Manchester in 1930 and qualified to be a doctor rather late in life in 1972. He immediately left England for Bangladesh. Having saved countless lives working miracles with the starving millions of that country, he was thrown out of Bangladesh after exposing a government racket involving the export of babies. He moved to Calcutta and became known as the Pavement Doctor. In the backstreets of Calcutta he treated the city's poor free of charge. His patients were destitute and dispossessed and would be suffering from tuberculosis and leprosy. Thousands came to see Dr Jack. On reading this book about the man I was so taken by him and his unusual story that I sent him a copy of *My Indian Journey*. Knowing the graphic details of his work in that city and having mixed with the poor there myself I felt I had something in common with him. I didn't really expect to get a reply, but I did. He wrote back to me very politely, saying he was reading my book with great enjoyment. I knew from his treasured letter that if I was ever to go to Calcutta again, he was one man I definitely wanted to meet. So one morning I asked Balaram if he knew of Dr Jack Preger. He replied that everyone in Calcutta knew of Dr Jack, so off we went in the taxi to find him.

Since his first clinic opened over 20 years ago, others had opened. Dr Jack could have been at any of them. That morning, Balaram took me to them all. Alas, no Dr Jack. The clinics are run by volunteers from abroad. Lots of British people go there for periods of six months. To support Dr Jack Preger a charity called Calcutta Rescue was formed. It raises money in various parts of the world to fund what it's achieving in Calcutta. Generous donations by good-hearted people support Calcutta Rescue. Without this generosity, Dr Jack and his staff would not be able to give this free treatment to the city's thousands of poor people.

Balaram looked everywhere for Dr Jack, without success. But I did get his home number from one of the clinics and that evening I rang him. I was told that Dr Jack was ill in bed with a fever and I couldn't possibly meet him.

"He really would love to meet you, but he's so ill he can't," I was told. So that was it - no way was I going to meet the famous Pavement Doctor of Calcutta. To say I was disappointed would be an understatement. I'd admired and respected him so much through reading that book. I felt that, in many respects, I knew him. In the book he admits to having committed enough sins in his life to merit a fair amount of punishment. His two broken marriages and two deserted children tell of a troubled personal life. He says he is no living saint, but to me he's one of life's heroes - a great character who can swear with the best of them and will literally take on anyone if he thinks he's right. He's upset the government of Calcutta so many times. They would love to clear him off the streets. I tell this short story of Jack Preger to illustrate that in the slums of this city there is a great Englishman. He was recently honoured by his Queen with a CBE. It was my great misfortune not to have met him.

One particular day Balaram took me to one of my favourite places in Calcutta, the Eden Gardens cricket ground. Last time I visited I'd begged the secretary in his office to let me in to the ground. "I've come all the way from England to see the Eden Gardens," I'd said. He relented and I was able to go to the centre of the ground for five minutes. This time, on inquiring at the office I was again allowed into the ground and stood in the stands. Now I don't know whether it was the dull weather, with no sun out, but it looked very different indeed. When last there I was struck by the place, in awe of it. Massive new stands had been put up and the sheer majesty and splendour of the ground took my breath away with its magnitude and vastness. I'd found my cathedral of cricket and I was in heaven. Well, it's heaven no more. I couldn't believe how shabby it looked. Before, it was as beautiful as Lord's cricket ground in London, but seeing what I did that day I wouldn't have believed it could have deteriorated in just five years. It looked really filthy. I'm sure a good paint job would have brought it back to its former glories. But as I stood in the stands that day I'd remembered that a year previously there had been a riot at the ground. Sri Lanka had beaten India in a World Cup match, 10,000 Indians were boiling over and the stands had been set alight. Much damage had been done, including some by fire. No wonder the ground looked shabby. I'm sure, though, that the weather didn't help at all that day. Everywhere looks so much better when the sun is out, but I came away from Eden Gardens cricket ground extremely disappointed in what I'd seen. I'd told cricket friends in England that it was the Taj Mahal of cricket. Now I'm not so sure. In many respects when I saw it that day for the second time it seemed to fit in most appropriately with the general decay and filth of a run-down city.

My last whole day in Calcutta was, to say the least, quite extraordinary in that I found what I'd been looking for. Each day I'd searched for a certain something. Would I find it, I kept asking myself. Why had I liked the city so much when I was last there? How could I have walked through this city, seen such degradation and actually enjoyed it? Hadn't I any feelings that first time? How could I possibly have mixed with the street kids of Calcutta and not been affected by their dreadful lives? Thousands of them are out on the streets, literally getting through each day on their wits' end through begging, thieving, scrounging and, from what I was told while in the city, child prostitution. Well, I was affected. So much so that when I arrived home I knew I would never be the same person again. Why was it that I was born into a middle-class Peterborough family with certain advantages? Why had I been singled out to come into this world to lead what was to some extent a life of privilege? Why, through an accident of birth, had I been born in England and not India? There seem to be so many unanswered questions as one gets older. Nobody need ever talk to me about the poor in my country, England, because in comparison to a good quarter of the world we just do not know what real poverty is. I know there are poor people in England, of course there are, and nobody's more sorry for them than me. But the poor I'm talking about are the very poorest of the poor. Out in the Third World there's such poverty that only those who have seen and witnessed it will know what I'm getting at. Just imagine you'd been born in the slums of Calcutta and not England. Just think also how horrific it would be waking up each day in some hell-hole with no food and water, and your children starving while your shockingly ill wife, the mother of your six children, is dying of malnutrition. You have sunk to the lowest depths. Even you yourself are coughing blood and retching on everything you eat (that's if you're lucky enough to eat) because your body is in a dreadful condition. You haven't worked for years because there is no work. All you are good for is begging in the streets. Your children are pleading with their hero - that's you - for food and your beautiful 12-year-old daughter, who is the absolute apple of your eye, is being persuaded by some pimp to turn to prostitution. How would the very thought of your darling sweet and innocent baby girl being molested by perverts affect you? Imagine seeing her at such a tender and vulnerable age trying to wear make-up and plying her trade on the streets. Her last words might be "don't worry about me, Daddy, I can take care of myself." And you, her father, are thinking "at least I'll be able to feed my other children when she comes home from her degrading work" even though her pimp might take 99 per cent of her measly earnings. Your darling little girl might come home with two black eyes and because she's been so badly sexually abused she can hardly walk. It would make any father go off his head, wouldn't it? But the family is so reliant on her money. Your baby girl cries every night, your sweet baby daughter who you bounced on your knee not so many years ago might well be dead at 18. You hate this pimp who is slowly murdering your daughter, but he might be your best friend because he's feeding your destitute family off your daughter's immoral earnings. That's what I call being poor. And there are millions living like that in India today. There are no social security payments, either. And me, how would I feel in this horrendous situation? I would probably say I wished I'd never been born.

And now to the City of Joy, or should I say The Real City of Joy. It was there that I found what I'd been looking for. How could anybody find joy in one of the most despicable places I've ever been to in my life? I'd found the modern-day Black Hole of Calcutta. Those who have read my previous book will remember me delving into the history of the Black Hole. In 1756 thousands of Indians attacked the British garrison of Fort William. Near the end of the most savage fighting, in which hundreds were killed, 145 English men and one woman were forced into a dungeon about the size of an English living room. It happened on the hottest night of the year. Because of the sheer heat and people having to literally sit on top of each other, many died through suffocation. Next day, when the doors to the dungeon were opened, just 22 people had survived. From then on this incident became known as The Black Hole of Calcutta. I tell this story again very briefly because in Calcutta today there are thousands of Black Holes, living human Black Holes. Thousands of the city's desperately poor live in intolerable, filthy and absolutely appalling conditions in little huts housing maybe 20 people.

So, on my last day in Calcutta I went to hell and back. I thought I was going through the gates of hell. This hell would have been scandalous in the London of Charles

Dickens' youth, and as my rickshaw puller eased his way down the narrowest of alleyways I wondered what on earth I'd let myself in for. I couldn't avoid wondering whether I was being brave or extremely foolish, but I'd regarded it as a challenge. I just had to see the greatest slum imaginable. Once in that rat-infested hole there was no escape. Come with me now into The Real City of Joy. I got what was very probably the surprise of my life there, but sitting in that rickshaw going into that slum I felt I was really going into the Black Hole of Calcutta.

My taxi driver, Balaram, was turning out to be a great guy, full of fun and with a great sense of humour. He spoke English reasonably well and because of his love of cricket we got on famously. That last day I asked him if he knew of The City of Joy. Sure enough, he did and told me that the film of the same name had been made at Howrah. So I asked if he would take me there. I had to have enough confidence in him, though, to form a bond of trust between us. I certainly didn't want him deserting me once I was inside the slum of all slums. I said I'd only go into this area provided he was with me the whole time. Sometimes one can only judge a person by looking straight into their face, and Balaram had an honest face. I was trusting him on face value alone, but I trusted him implicitly. So, off we went once again through the streets of Calcutta and for the first time we crossed the River Houghly, by the massively ugly metal Howrah Bridge. It is right in the heart of the city, so thousands of people cross it every day. Although I say ugly bridge, which it is, it also has a great presence and Calcutta wouldn't be the same without it. Built by the British of 60 years ago and still standing, it is a real feat of engineering. Once over the bridge I noticed an immediate deterioration in the area we were travelling through. I was now in the district of Howrah, which of course is still part of Calcutta. Through that taxi window I could see the beggars were waiting for me and the pavement-dwellers, those people who sleep on the streets, seemed to have woken up to see this man from afar. We really were in a slum. Call it a shanty town if you like, but a slum is a slum. Whole crowds of Calcutta's poor had gathered around the taxi. Goodness knows how many hundreds of them there were. Balaram then told me we would have to get a rickshaw because the alleyways were too narrow for his taxi to get through. We jumped on the first rickshaw and the poor man pulling it looked as thin as a rake. As the rickshaw pulled away, many eyes never left me. I felt I was being looked at all over. I'd asked Balaram to come with me because I literally didn't know what to expect. If things got nasty at least I'd have him by my side, and he could also speak the language. But could I bear what I was about to see? What effect would it have on me? I was full of apprehension - 300,000 homeless people live out their lives in the Howrath district. I was in the neighbourhood of Anand Nager, known in English as The City of Joy. I had arrived in hell. What kind of greeting was I likely to get, I wondered.

Dominique Lapierre's masterpiece of a best-selling story was coming to life right before my eyes. Can anyone from the Western world possibly imagine 70,000 people crowding into an area twice the size of a football stadium, living in little mud huts? Imagine 10 people trying to bed down in a garden shed. Those poor slum dwellers looked so undernourished that I couldn't begin to describe the appearance of some of them. I kept asking myself how people could live here. The children, some suffering from malnutrition for the want of a good meal, some with clothes on and some with no clothes at all, all stared at this man passing among them. The rickshaw made its way very slowly through such appalling squalor that it's difficult for me to find the correct words to describe it. My feelings were playing up again. What must the sanitation be like here?

Were there proper toilets? Would they have clean running water? How would they eat? The summer heat must be a real killer, with temperatures getting to over 100 degrees. This slum must be one of the unhealthiest places on earth. What disease must there be in those huts? What must it be like when the rains come, when whole areas are flooded? With no money, how would they survive? I thought of the countless rats. I thought of huge cockroaches, the degradation, the smells, people somehow surviving in stinking filth, the early deaths that must take place here, and, yes, the diseases. I could go on. My comfortable life in England seemed a million miles away. How do inhabitants of this rat hole of a slum live out their lives under such contemptible conditions? I'd never seen anything to compare with it - those little huts huddled together like cowsheds either side of our rickshaw, with people expected to live their lives there. What hopelessness there was there. I sat in that rickshaw with Balaram in a complete daze. Down these little alleyways we went. I was in some sort of hell. I just knew I could never possibly forget what I was seeing.

Halfway round this slum of all slums I asked the rickshaw puller to stop. I reached for my camera and started taking photographs. I got off the rickshaw and suddenly everything changed. One second I was in the very depths of depression and the next all was smiles and laughter. The whole atmosphere was transformed. I wouldn't have believed it could have happened. Those hundreds of people who had been leaning out of their huts to see me and the children who had been following me all started laughing. All kids, wherever they may be, love to be photographed and these were getting so excited at me taking their picture. All at once the bustee-dwellers were all smiles. Before, they had looked at me with suspicion and curiosity, but everything had changed. The more I laughed, the more everyone else laughed. This wasn't hell, I thought. People just wouldn't be laughing in hell. I knew from that very moment that I'd found the real City of Joy that Dominique Lapierre had found. While researching for the writing of his book, this Frenchman found so much heroism, so much love, so much happiness, so much sharing amidst so much ugliness and darkness. The quite staggering thing was that he found people who possessed absolutely nothing, yet seemed to have everything. For six months he'd lived with these people in order to write his book, a book that snatches and pulls at your heart strings from the very first page. I was simply overwhelmed by it. It was a book of dramas and unforgettable human emotions. Lapierre's neighbours were eunuchs and the local mafia. There was even a leper colony in the slum. And here was I reliving that book. Those children were so pleased to see me that I knew I was with the street kids of Calcutta again, as I had been before. I'd found what I'd been looking for. This was why I'd enjoyed Calcutta so much when last in the city. I'd mixed with them out on the streets. I'd loved being with them, these street kids who were so despised by the high and middle castes of this incredible city. I'd felt so sorry for them, I'd made friends with them and I'd left them to their pathetic lives. This is what I'd missed. Although I'd promised my family I wouldn't go out alone in the city, I'd missed its soul, the very heart of the place, and by going into that slum I'd found it again. And, as I came away from the City of Joy having travelled round it for two hours in that rickshaw, the slum-dwellers were waving at me and laughing. I was definitely laughing. I'd been to the very depths of degradation, but I'd found such happiness there. This was not hell that I'd found. It might even have been heaven. I'd found such joy there - far more than one might find in the more affluent West.

Just before we left the slum area of Howrah we visited

a clinic run by Dr Anjan K. Kar, he being part of a team who treat children with malnutrition. He is a specialist in maternal and child diseases, his clinic is open every day and hundreds of children are in his care. Many will die through lack of good food. The disease most rampant here, among many others, is tuberculosis. I took an instant liking to this doctor and he had a wonderful sense of humour. He took me to see one of his wards, where the seriously ill children are - many of them just babies.

Here I was to meet an Indian nurse with the Welsh name of Alice John, who was in charge of the ward. Her love for those undernourished children, caring for them as though they were her own, was a joy to see. What love, what dedication, I thought. How could these poor souls in Howrah survive without this doctor and his very caring nurse, together with the other nurses and helpers? These people were giving their lives to India's poor. I'm sure hundreds - maybe thousands - of babies on the verge of death have been saved in this clinic. Dr Kar's job is to treat children with tuberculosis. Other diseases which would be quite common here would include cholera, dysentery and diphtheria to name but a few.

Balaram, who had never left my side, then told the doctor I used to play cricket.

"You played cricket? Why didn't you tell me," he shouted excitedly. I knew I'd found another friend. Immediately, because of cricket, there was a bond between us. At this particular time I was sitting at his office desk. He wanted to know what I was doing in India and seemed most interested in the book I'd written after my stay five years earlier.

"You mention your book, but did you know that Dominique Lapierre sat in that very chair you are sitting in right now when he first came to see me while researching his book *The City of Joy*", the doctor said. I remember replying that unfortunately my book would never become a number one best seller like Dominique Lapierre's. The doctor then said, without a moment's hesitation:

"Well, he's a Frenchman, isn't he, and much cleverer than you."

"What do you mean he's cleverer than me?" I said.

"Being French he must be cleverer than you," he replied.

"Are you saying that he's cleverer than me because he's French?" I asked.

"Well, he is, isn't he, with you not being very clever," said the doctor, now chuckling.

"Thank you very much," I said.

"This Frenchman is a very clever man indeed," the doctor said, laughing.

"How can a Frenchman be cleverer than me, an Englishman?" says I, both of us now laughing.

"He's cleverer than you because you are not very bright," said the doctor, now splitting his sides.

"Are you saying I'm not very bright?" I persisted, now also in stitches.

"Yes, I am," he said. Loud laughter roared round that office. This doctor's brown face was turning red. He thought it all so funny. I thought it was hilarious.

"In fact he's so much cleverer than you. You're not very bright at all," said the doctor again. This really was getting ridiculous, with both of trying to regain our composure. And still, amidst much laughter, he said: "Let me examine you." He then proceeded to give me a near full medical examination in a most farcical manner, even using his stethoscope on my chest.

"You're in great shape and your heart is very good. Nothing wrong with you," he said.

At this stage in the proceedings I began to think that the doctor had far more deserving cases than me to examine. He reminded me of a Peter Sellers film, where Sellers plays the part of an Indian doctor. I'd found a marvellously funny doctor in the City of Joy. Our laughter often bordered on the ridiculous. Here was I in an absolutely appalling slum, a modern-day Black Hole, being hysterical with laughter and enjoying humour that I certainly didn't think I could possibly have found.

After an hour or so he escorted me, with Nurse Alice John, to the front door of his clinic with these words: "Mr Brian, your book. Please send one to me, won't you? I've read Dominique Lapierre's book. He's a famous writer, but I want to read your book because you will never be famous... you not being very bright." He chuckled again at that last part.

"Goodbye, Mr Brian. It was a pleasure to have met you," he said as we shook hands. But the pleasure was all mine. I'm sure Dr Kar has played his part in making the City of Joy a better place to live in, not only with his medicine but also with his outrageous humour, and as that rickshaw pulled out of the place called Anand Nager, where I'd found poverty the like of which I'd never seen before or am ever likely to see again, I looked back on a few hours that had been really unbelievable. The happiness I'd found there took my breath away. How could people be so happy amidst such misery? I'd gone in there with certain reservations, wondering not so much about what I was going to see but whether those slum-dwellers would accept me. I need not have worried. I was accepted with open arms. I'm sure they were pleased to see me because the welcome I received was simply overwhelming. India has all too often surprised me and I'm sure it will continue to do so. That day visiting Anand Nager would be imprinted on my mind forever.

Chapter Three

Return to Tongo

When the Indian Airways aircraft landed at Ranchi Airport from Calcutta the flight had taken just 45 minutes. I was once again in the north eastern state of Bihar, the most backward, violent and corrupt state in all India. Things hadn't improved since I was last there. Certain parts of this state are now classed as terrorist areas. White people, myself included, were told to exercise extreme caution if going there and to stay away completely if at all possible. I was well and truly in bandit country again. That is what Bihar is known as, with gangs of thugs openly causing terror and defying the law. Murders are an everyday occurrence and the police have little control. Often they themselves are corrupt, deliberately turning a blind eye to what's going on. Evidently, it's difficult to find anybody who's a somebody who is not corrupt. It seems to be accepted that corruption is part and parcel of Indian life. Society is riddled with it. Everyone has a price, most are on the make, or should I say take, and the politicians are in the thick of it. Even the former prime minister, in office only months ago, is up on corruption charges. As I stepped off that plane I was again full of apprehension. But I'd been in this state before and felt reasonably safe. There was very little violence in the Tongo area near Bihar and I knew I'd be in safe hands and well looked after by the Ursuline sisters, and once out in the sunshine and off the plane my thoughts were not of the violence of the state but whether anyone would be at the airport to meet me.

When the aircraft had touched down I'd looked through the little side windows to see if I could see anyone. When last there I could see Sister Bernadette and Albina on the airport roof. This time I couldn't see anyone and as I walked into the small terminal building I'd looked up to see if anyone was at the windows waving to me, but alas there was no one. I was convinced there was no one there to meet me. Obviously the sisters and Albina hadn't received my message from Calcutta. I resigned myself to having to make my own way to the Ranchi Ursuline convent school and hoped I'd be told of any new arrangements there. Because of my lateness the Ursuline sisters had perhaps had to return to Tongo and Albina to her teaching position at a place called Bihar Sharif, which was approximately 70 miles from Ranchi.

But I was wrong. Inside the airport building were many smiling faces, everyone with garlands of flowers in their hands and waiting to greet me. I immediately embraced Sister Vianney and also there was Sister Bernadette Tete, who had travelled from Dorma convent school that morning. I was also introduced to the new principal of the Tongo school, Sister Margaret Mary. There was quite a crowd at the airport, including some children I didn't recognise. What a welcome I was getting, being garlanded with all these flowers. Then I saw Albina Kujur, who had deliberately held back. "Greetings, Papa," she said, as even more garlands were put around my neck. My sponsored child that was looked extremely attractive in her pink sari. She was by now 27 years old and looked a very confident young lady. I noticed immediately that her English was much better than before. She was now able to speak the language well and I looked forward to many conversations with her. She was a school teacher, a position of some importance in India. This lower-caste girl from the tribe of Oron in south Bihar had achieved her ambition. She was indeed a some-body, and I was also very proud of her.

Somehow the whole crowd of us - and there must

have been 15 people including the children - managed to climb into a very small ambulance standing outside the airport building. This ambulance was in a dreadful condition and it simply rattled along as we made our way through the never-ending mass of traffic in the crowded streets of Ranchi. I shall never forget being repeatedly surprised by the sheer spectacle of thousands of people on Indian city streets. Ranchi has a population of 500,000 people. It bulges at the seams and is constantly at overflowing level. Although it is much smaller than Calcutta I'm sure there are more people per square mile in Ranchi. In terms of geographical area it is probably about the size of an English town of about 20,000 people, yet hundreds of thousands live there. Amid the hustle and bustle are thousands of rickshaws, mostly the pedal cycle variety, whereas in Calcutta they are man-drawn. Also in the streets are cars, lorries, buses, the smells and the beggars and of course the sacred cow of Hinduism. India certainly wouldn't be the same without it.

At the Ranchi convent school I'd had a talk with Sister Bernadette. She, of course, was the headmistress of the Tongo school when I first came to India and was also the one who had invited me to visit the school for as long as I wished. Having left Tongo, she was now in semi-retirement, teaching at the Ursuline convent school at Dorma, which is only a few miles from Ranchi. But her ambition had been to return to her home village of Gotra, even more southerly in Bihar than Tongo. It had been arranged that during my stay in Tongo I would visit her there. Sister Bernadette told me that under no circumstances was I to go to Bihar Sharif, which was where Albina was teaching.

"It has been declared a terrorist area by the government. Please do not go. Your life will be in danger. You would be an easy target for kidnapping," Sister Bernadette had warned. I had set my heart on visiting Bihar Sharif. I wanted so much to see the school where Albina was teaching. I'd have given anything to see her teaching her pupils and also to see where she was living and the area, and to meet her friends. My idea was to spend three days with her at her school. I reluctantly yielded to Sister Bernadette's request. I was well aware that five Westerners had been kidnapped in north India just a year before my return to the country. One body had been recovered by the police. This Westerner, who was Dutch, had been beheaded. Nothing has been heard for months now about the other four hostages, two of them Britons. Their families were in India at the same time as I was, appealing on TV for information about their loved ones. Were they alive or dead, they wanted to know. Say I'd gone to Bihar Sharif and been kidnapped. Being white, I'd be an easy target. I couldn't possibly put my wife and family through an ordeal like that. It's bad enough for relatives if their loved ones have been murdered, but to have no information at all is so cruel. Just think - not knowing whether your husband is still alive and being kept prisoner in some despicable place or dead. Nevertheless, I was still very disappointed at not going to Bihar Sharif.

After meeting me at Ranchi, Sister Bernadette had to make her own way back to Dorma. We also left behind Albina's brother John Kujur and his two daughters of eight and six, who lived in Ranchi. After we had a quick meal at the school, the ambulance made its way out of Ranchi on the Thursday and Albina had until the Monday before she had to return to her school, so hopefully I would be seeing quite a lot of her. It was decided that we should make for Tongo that afternoon, but it would be well into the evening by the time we arrived. It was only 30 miles, but 30 miles over some of the most dreadful roads imaginable is something else. Those roads are deplorable, with potholes galore.

I was being thrown from side to side in the ambulance, which incidentally was getting more temperamental than ever - a real old banger. Sometimes we could only go at 10 mph. We even had to leave the road on some occasions because it became impassable and rejoin it 20 yards or so later. By late afternoon it was getting dark and out in the subcontinent it really is dark, pitch black like a blanket in front of you. Just as it was getting dark we approached a bridge which had been completely swept away by floods. Fortunately the river was by now dry and we managed to cross it. Eventually we made it to the town of Gumla. The ambulance had just about packed up and a motor mechanic had to be found. The gearbox was in a poor way, but, managing on temporary repairs, we chugged off again. Would we reach Tongo, I began to wonder.

With there being no lighting along the countryside roads, I began to notice that the ambulance's own lights were fading. If that vehicle had broken down we would definitely have spent the night there. We wouldn't have left the ambulance either. Wild animals are know to roam about at night. It really was the slowest journey imaginable. By the time we finally approached the village of Tongo it had taken six hours to travel 30 miles. My back was, by then, giving me some stick. The constant banging of being thrown up and down had put great pressure on my back and it was really hurting at the base. It all reminded me so much of what had happened the last time I was at Tongo. For many days I had scarcely been able to move. What relief I felt, therefore, as we pulled up outside the brand new gates of the school wall. After a few minutes of blowing the ambulance's horn the gates were opened and we went into the school grounds. I was once again in the place I'd so desperately needed to return to. Part of me had never left that school. On climbing out of the ambulance, the first person to greet me was Sister

Michael, "Auntie". I called her this because that's exactly how I saw her, forever fussing round me when I was there before, just like some auntie might do for an affectionate nephew. All the Ursuline sisters had come out to meet me. The school children, all of them boarders at the school, started singing. This was what I'd longed to hear. Their singing had such an effect on me. It radiates so much of the happiness that's found at the school. Surely there couldn't be another school like it anywhere. So, after much singing and many greetings, I was ushered into the residence where the sisters live.

A meal had been prepared for me in the dining room and being with the Divine Sisters of Tongo again it was as though I had never been away from them. There was much laughter around that table. The humour of the sisters was shining through, that humour I'd thought about so many times over the years. I was with some very special friends again. Their love and devotion to God and the school children was a joy to behold. God is there in everything they are involved with. These brides of Christ would forever be telling me that if it is God's will, it will be done. They spoke this way five years ago. Even in letters sent to me over the years they repeated this belief. Sister Bernadette always wrote to me saying that if it was God's will the wall would be repaired. It was always God's will, irrespective of whether it was good news or bad. And here I was at the dining table, which was just as I'd remembered it. Things hadn't changed much. Power cuts were still happening. As we sat talking by oil lamp, I looked around that table. Lots of friends who I'd thought about so many times were latching on to my every word. They included Sister Michael, Sister Vianney, Sister Scholastica, Sister Josephine, Sister Alphonsa, Sister Frederic, Sister Terisita and Sister Armit. All these sisters had been here five years ago, but other old friends had been moved on to other convent schools. They included Sister Albina, Sister Bernadette, Sister Sushila, Sister Arrivita, Sister Anna, Sister Goretti, Sister Maxima and Sister Angela. I would particularly miss Sister Sushila because it was she who would massage my back every evening when I was in such pain. I knew I would miss all of them, but that evening I quickly got talking to the new sisters, who seemed to have fitted in perfectly, and I was looking forward to making new friendships. I look upon the Divine Sisters of Tongo as some of the best friends I've ever made in my life. Their love for me was returned by my love for them. Because of that love I had to get that school wall repaired. I had to protect them. The school is now secure. I realise that if someone really wanted to break in, nothing would keep them out, but it certainly wouldn't be as easy as it was before.

That first evening with the sisters, they told me they were on strike, starting the very day of my arrival. I knew there was the possibility of a strike because Sister Vianney had written to me about it. Apparently the Ursuline sisters of Bihar hadn't been paid for the last 18 months.There are more than 500 Ursuline sisters in Bihar, including state school teachers, and they hadn't been paid. This sad state of affairs applied only to senior schools. Literally hundreds of schools would be closed down. This was to be no ordinary strike. It was a hunger strike. It was called to start that day, purely to get the chief government minister of Bihar to change his mind. Sister Sarita, one of the newer sisters at Tongo, would represent the school as she and other Ursuline sisters and school teachers from Bihar would camp outside the chief minister's home at Patna, in north Bihar. They would stay there until he changed his mind. They would not eat anything during this time.

I remember saying: "How on earth can nuns go on hunger strike? Surely it is against all Christian beliefs. It is suicide." The sisters told me something had to be done.

The chief government minister was not paying their wages and how could they survive at the school without pay? The money they earn is not for themselves. Their wages go toward meeting the general running costs of the school, so how could it stay open with no money coming in? There were also teachers living in Tongo village who were affected by the strike and from that first day senior school pupils were told not to attend school, as there would be no one there to teach them. I remember thinking long and hard about what I was about to say.

"But surely you wouldn't starve yourselves to death. This is a great sin," I said.

"Mr Brian, it's our last resort. Don't ask me if Sister Sarita and the other sisters will starve themselves to death. We hope it doesn't come to that, but we have to be strong and support the strike. Hopefully we can get some publicity and the chief minister will give in. He's not going to like hundreds of people camping outside his house every day and night, is he?" said Sister Michael.

"Why won't he pay your wages?" I asked.

"Probably another corrupt politician," said another sister's voice further down that long dining table. I was also told it was a particularly bad time of year for a strike, with the year-end exams coming up. My sympathies were obviously with the sisters, but it could also be said - and I think it is a more likely answer that that offered by the sisters - that the state of Bihar is bankrupt. This wouldn't surprise me at all.

"We have no alternative. We have to strike," said the sisters with one voice. I was then told that the chief government minister had broken his leg. This being the man who has unlimited control over virtually everything which goes on in Bihar. I sensed a touch of humour about this around the table. I kept a straight face as I asked how he had broken his leg. Evidently he had slipped on the floor at his home. I started thinking about everything in the sisters' lives being God's will.

"Well, that's God's will then, isn't it? Perhaps that's God's way of punishing him for not paying your wages," I said. The sisters were now looking at me in a most peculiar way, but I continued to keep a straight face. "Surely you must have sympathy for someone who has broken his leg," I said. The looks I was getting from the sisters said "Whose side are you on - ours or the chief minister's?"

"The poor man, hobbling around all day on one leg," I persisted. Suddenly I couldn't keep a straight face any longer and burst out laughing. Then the sisters laughed, more out of relief than anything, I think. The look on their faces told me they certainly didn't have too much sympathy for the chief government minister and his broken leg. He was not paying their wages and they were none too pleased with him.

We all went upstairs, laughing all the way to our bedrooms, at 8.30pm. The electricity was on again, though by 9pm it would definitely be off, so everyone had to be in bed by that time. I'd been given the same room as before. It looked quite comfy and familiar, and once under my mosquito net I was hoping for a good night's sleep. I thought of my family. I felt millions of miles away from them. I was once again in the back of beyond. England seemed a world away. Once the lights were out I was well and truly in deepest Bihar and everywhere was so quiet. I remember thinking how peaceful it was. I was just drifting off when the most hideous howling noises imaginable started. It was the dogs. I'd never in all my life come across barking like it, the most peculiar noises I'd ever heard - some barking, some yapping, mixed with groaning and moaning, some snarling and some crying. Yes, dogs crying. These hideous howling noises went on well into the night. I thought some of them were noises a dog couldn't possibly make. I convinced myself there must have been 50 dogs out there. Lying in that bed that first night, all kinds of different things started going through my mind. Having read so much about the violence in Bihar and that law and order had completely broken down there, I even thought about the Bihar bandits, as they are known. Were they trying to break into the school? Obviously something was disturbing the dogs. I also knew that police are just not seen in the Tongo area of Bihar, so there would be no protection. I also knew that being white and English I was in an extremely vulnerable position. These bandits kill indiscriminately and ask questions later. I hardly slept at all, thinking about what might happen. I was more than thankful when the early morning light started coming through my bedroom window. One thinks differently in the daylight and I was grateful for it. In the darkness of Bihar things can happen to one's mind. I knew I had the love and protection of the Ursuline sisters while I was with them at Tongo, but in all honesty their protection wouldn't have amounted to much if the Bihar bandits had raided that convent school. I would literally have been on my own. These gangs are nothing more than criminals. Their notoriety spreads throughout North Bihar and the police seem to be nonexistent. The gangs seem to have them in their pocket. But I'd got through my first night in Bihar and hopefully I would be more ready and alert when those animal noises, or whatever other noises I might hear while lying on my bed, started up again on another night. But I had quickly come to the conclusion that I was right in the very heart of India, a lone English tourist out in the wilds of the sub-continent.

I had to accept, therefore, that I was not in England any more. I had forsaken the country of my birth to return to India. It was my decision entirely, certainly no one else's, to return to the state of Bihar. This was the country I had been so determined to return to. What else did I expect? I had to accept the consequences and that anything might happen. For five years I had dreamt of returning. At times I'd thought of little else. In many respects it had dominated my life. Indeed my wife had said that India had actually taken over my life. In many respect she was right. I knew while lying in that bed on that first night, being kept awake by some of the strangest noises I'd ever heard, that I hadn't exactly been fair to my wife. In my obsession with helping India I'd probably neglected her. It couldn't have been easy for her seeing me going out sometimes three nights a week to speak of India to some group of people 40 miles away. I had become so involved in raising money for Tongo. Yes, while lying on that bed I thought of my wife. But she also knew how important my return to Tongo was to me. So whatever was happening on the other side of that convent wall on that first night, I had asked for it. Having read so much about India in those five years I had to accept that there was a certain danger in returning. But having said that, it was also very exciting to be back at that school again. I had returned to Tongo. I had dreamt of it so many times and now my dream was complete.

Next morning at the breakfast table I mentioned the barking to the sisters. "What disturbed all those dogs?" I remember asking. "It seemed as though someone was trying to break in," I said.

"No break-in here last night," said Sister Scholastica.

"It could be the rats causing the dogs to bark," said Sister Michael.

"When I was here last you told me there were no rats here," I said.

"During the day that's true, but at night we are overrun by them. They come in every night from the forests. This place is swarming with them. They come up the drainpipes and get on the roof. We lie in bed and we can hear them. They keep us awake sometimes, particularly when they start squeaking - the dear little things," said Sister Michael.

Oh God, I thought. If there are two things I fear in life, they are plane flights and rats. There would certainly be no window open in my room at night time any more. I shuddered at the thought of being surrounded by rats at night. I could even imagine them staring at me and scratching the glass as they sat on my bedroom window sill.

When I was having my injections at my local health centre before going to India I inquired if I could have any protection against a rat bite. The reason I'd asked was that about three years ago in one of the northern states of India there had been an earthquake. Millions of rats had been disturbed and were on the move. India really is a rat-infested country and the ones that had been disturbed carried a particular flea on them and if that flea landed on a human being, the person would be dead within hours. Because of this, more than 1,000 people had died. I had been told at the health centre that my chances of being bitten by a rat or indeed catching something from one were very remote - a million to one, in fact - and there was no cause for alarm. Consequently I did not have any additional injections. All these thoughts were going through my head as I sat at the breakfast table. I certainly couldn't do anything about the situation and it rather put me off my breakfast. All I could think about was rats.

After breakfast I went for a short walk with Sister Scholastica, the headmistress of the junior school. I know I shall never be able to pronounce her name. We turned left at the main gates and within minutes I was in the most beautiful and colourful countryside it has ever been my pleasure to see. The beauty of Bihar takes one's breath away. The school is on a slight hill and the scenery is quite spectacular. The land is a lovely mixture of green and gold. Everything seemed to be coming to life again after the monsoon, which would only have finished about a month before. The sun always seems to shine in Bihar, and it gives everything a startling brightness. The hills, the valleys, the streams and the forests can all be seen from that hilltop. I could literally see for miles. The feeling I got that morning was of being completely overwhelmed by the sheer beauty before my eyes. I also felt extremely fortunate to be standing on that hill. I don't suppose too many white people have ever been to that part of Bihar anyway. I was indeed the privileged one and I'd once again found the most idyllic spot imaginable. Standing with Sister Scholastica on that hill I could see the little groups of children making their way to school, little five and six-year-olds who were chattering in their excitement having set off from villages many miles away. Lots of different age groups of junior children were coming in from all directions. These children would walk miles every morning to come to school, whatever their ages. Sometimes the group passing us would be 30-strong and on greeting me they would place their hands together in front of their faces and say "Namaste", which means greetings. This most courteous of Hindu gestures is practised all over Tongo - a real Indian custom. One can imagine the number of times I was given greetings by all the different groups of children as they came to school. Sister Scholastica had said how much everyone at the school had looked forward to my visit. I also knew that on that particular day there was going to be quite a welcome from the whole school.

My first whole day back at the school was one of constant celebration. Wherever I went it was "Greetings", not only from the sisters but also the teachers and junior school children. There was not a single senior pupil at the school because of the strike. They were bending over backwards in their welcome for me. I knew I'd helped in raising money to repair the wall, but in all honesty I didn't think I'd done anything special. It was no big deal. I'd just done something I'd wanted to do anyway, so I didn't feel I should take undue credit for it. The enjoyment of raising the money was to me one of the most pleasurable experiences I've ever had. Sister Michael had said I'd been sent to India for a purpose - a mission, she called it. She had come into that same Tongo bedroom of mine five years ago and said, when I was lying there in great pain from my back:

"You have been sent to us, Mr Brian." I remember asking her what she meant.

"You remember what I say. You have been sent here for a purpose. You have been sent here on a mission," she said. As I was in such terrible pain I didn't take too much notice of what she was saying at the time, but once I was home in England, her words came to me many times and I know from subsequent experience that what she said was true, so I didn't feel I should be taking credit for something I was sent to India to do. On arriving home that first time I knew I couldn't fail the sisters and the school children. I was being pushed in the strangest of ways and it's something that even now I find difficult to explain. But I'd got the message from Sister Michael and that message was to help the school, and here I was being repaid for what I'd done. I didn't want any celebrations, I just wanted to return to the school to see that wall, so I was somewhat embarrassed by the welcome I was getting. And what a welcome. Children seemed to be singing all over the school and I was forever being garlanded with flowers as I made my way with the sisters into the school hall. Once in the hall, the real singing started and I was once again in the world of The Sound of Music.

There were 700 junior school children in that hall and music is very much in their blood. They were displaying their sheer joy of singing and dancing on the school stage for my benefit. These children, who come from some of the poorest homes imaginable, were so pleased to see me. After about one-and-a-half hours the music stopped. Speeches were made and I was then escorted by the sisters, with the children following on behind, to the site of the new school building, which houses six additional classrooms. After the wall was repaired I continued to send money to the school and with more financial help from a lady in Belgium these extra classrooms were built. Standing in front of the building that day looking at it, it was quite magnificent. If it had been built in England it would have cost at least £80,000, but in India building costs are considerably lower. The village priest of Tongo welcomed me to the building and then a short service took place as he blessed each classroom. I was then asked to cut the tape and the building was official opened amidst much clapping from the children. On being taken round the classrooms by the priest and the sisters I noticed they were all unfurnished, so school furniture was definitely needed. Without it, the children were sitting on the floor. But they looked so excited to be in their new school building at last and I was only too pleased to be there with them, because these classrooms were so badly needed. There really are not enough schools for Indian children, but thankfully the Tongo school is growing and that means that even more children from the countryside will be getting an education.

Later that afternoon I was taken all the way round the school wall by Sister Vianney. It probably stretches for nearly a mile. A good half of it was down when I was last there, but it is now looking strong and secure. In fact, I thought it looked quite indestructible, and the new iron gates gave it a look of total security. While walking around that wall I couldn't help but think of all the people who'd helped me repair it. I was so thankful to everyone who bought the *My Indian Journey* book, for the donations given by endless groups of people who heard me speak and to all those good people who sponsored me for the London Marathon. Literally thousands of people had helped repair that wall. If only people in England, particularly those in the Deepings, where I live, could have seen it, because without such help, nothing could have been done. Countless people in my local area have stopped me in the street over the past five years to ask "How's the wall going?" At least by writing *India Revisited* I'm able to bring my whole Indian experience up to date. I also noticed while walking around the school how much it had deteriorated. It looked quite shabby. A coat of paint would have helped. Large cracks were appearing in the walls of the buildings and a lot of work was needed. If only I could raise even more money to carry out those repairs. The school was in decay and it hurt. I know it gets help from the Indian government, but it is not nearly enough. It's as though the government's point of view is that as long as the school is functioning, all must be well. Surveying the whole Tongo school that day, I had my own little dream, a vision if you like, that I must continue to raise money for the school. I began to form a Golden Vision of what might be. I can only do it if people in England support me. I'm hoping that from the sales of this book I can continue to help the school. I'm also hoping that when those groups I have spoken to know I have returned to India and come home with another story they will want me to speak to them again.

That evening at the dining table I gave the sisters the piano music of The Sound of Music, which I'd brought with me from England. I had seen this music book in a shop locally and thought immediately of the sisters and Tongo. I told the sisters about the very successful stage show and film and said the popularity of the music would live forever. To me it was one of the greatest - if not *the* greatest - musical films ever made. I told them how much the school reminded me of the film, which although shot in Austria included some scenes set in a convent. I thought the Ursuline sisters at Tongo would be most interested, but they confessed to never having heard of it. That really surprised me - I thought The Sound of Music was known worldwide. I also found to my disappointment that there was no piano at the school - all those fine musical school children and not a single piano in Tongo. They didn't have any other musical instruments either. The only instruments I remember seeing were drums. On talking to the sisters about the film, they gave me the shock of my life by asking me to sing one of the songs.

"I've never sung to anyone," I remember saying, but then I surprised myself by singing Climb Every Mountain. This was quite an effort on my part, believe me. The sisters listened and no one laughed, which was a relief. They actually said they'd enjoyed it. I have this song on tape in my car and I'm forever playing it because it reminds me so much of Tongo. Climb Every Mountain, Follow your Dream. Those words came to sum up for me why I wanted to help the school. On some of my car journeys to speak about India I would play this tape over and over again. It's as though I've never tired of it. It was indeed my inspiration and wherever I was speaking I always felt more than capable of giving a reasonable talk and slide show. Because of that song, it didn't matter how many people were waiting for me as I walked into a hall somewhere and extra-large attendances often brought out the best in me. And here I was, telling the sisters about those wonderful songs, and because they hadn't got a piano, the music would never be heard. The crying shame is that Tongo is a school full of music. Music really is in the blood of these Indian school children. They love to sing and to dance and whenever I walked through the school, there always seemed to be a classroom breaking into song. I know it would have been practically impossible for me to have transported some old broken-down piano out to Tongo, but if it could have been done that piano would have become the prize possession of the school. If I close my eyes I can visualise 1300 Indian school children singing the music from that film, their beautiful voices flowing through the oh-so-colourful countryside of southern Bihar, with the sloping hills in the distance. The song The Hills are Alive with the Sound of Music would have fitted in perfectly with that scene at Tongo and I can assure you that no school children anywhere could have sung it any better. One only has to look at the sheer happiness of the children to see the truth in that. So, Climb Every Mountain was my dream song for Tongo and I can only dream that one day those songs might well be sung there.

Chapter Four

Sister Bernadette's Dream

Sister Bernadette Tete was the headmistress of the senior school at Tongo in the district of Gumla when I first visited it. It was really because of her that I went to India. I'd written to her at Christmas 1990 asking her to inform me of the whereabouts of a girl I'd sponsored called Albina Kujur. I'd sponsored this girl from the age of 11 through the charity ActionAid. Through my paying the charity a very small monthly amount of money, this girl was able to have an education which she would not otherwise have received. I helped her from 1978 to 1988. I might add here that literally thousands of children in the Third World are being given an education through sponsorship. Thousands of people in the West are sponsoring children this way, ActionAid being just one of the charities throughout the world that allow them to do so.

Albina wrote me many letters during those 10 years and I realised very early that here was no ordinary girl. Her ambition was to go to college and become a school teacher. This was some ambition for a poor girl born into the lower caste of Indian society. But all at once her letters to me stopped and ActionAid wrote to me saying the sponsorship programme for Albina had finished because she was by then above the required age for it. I couldn't sponsor her any more. I wrote pleading letters to ActionAid telling them I wanted to continue helping this girl. I knew how important it was for her to go to college. ActionAid wrote back saying they couldn't help. I wrote to the school at Tongo, where she was a pupil and where she also lived, but I didn't get a reply. As I didn't have an address for Albina's family and all my letters went to the school, it looked very much as if

I'd lost her.

So when I wrote to the headmistress at Tongo at Christmas 1990 I certainly wasn't sure I'd get a reply. Two years had passed and I thought I'd write one final letter. "Please tell me what has happened to Albina Kujur," I wrote. Three months later a letter arrived from Tongo written by the Ursuline sister who was then headmistress of the school. Her name was Sister Bernadette Tete. In her letter she told me Albina was alive and well and attending a college in Bihar, where she hoped to pass her exams to become a school teacher. Sister Bernadette also gave me a pressing invitation to visit the school, stay as long as I wanted, and meet Albina. Well, the rest is history. I went to India and met Albina, so when I arrived in India for the second time to be met at Ranchi Airport by, among others, Sister Bernadette, I felt somewhat indebted to her. Two years previously she had gone into semi-retirement. She was 65 and had to relinquish her position as headmistress. She was moved on to an Ursuline convent school called Dorma, which is near Ranchi. Evidently, although she taught occasionally at Dorma, she missed being involved full-time, having travelled in many areas of Bihar and been involved with many of the Ursuline schools all over the state. As she got nearer to the age of 65, she wanted increasingly to return to the area of her birth, so, a few months before I arrived in India for the second time, she had made a decision to return to the village where she was born. The name of the village was Gotra, which is right at the southern end of Bihar, in the subdivision of Simdega in the district of Gujla. The area borders the state of Orrisa and it is even more remote than Tongo. The main reason Sister Bernadette wanted to go back there was that she had a dream - to build a hospital in the village of her birth.

Sister Bernadette's ambition was to return to her home village, build a hospital, live out her remaining years there and die there. About a year before my return to India she had written to me, telling me of her dream. In fact she wrote several letters about it. As I'd always kept in written contact with her during the last five years, it was not unusual for her to share it with me. But for her dream to be realised, thousands of pounds were going to have to be raised. Could I help by raising money for this Gotra hospital in England, she asked in her letters. She was pleading with me to help. A medical centre was so desperately needed in that part of India.

"People are dying through lack of medical help," she wrote. "Please help. This hospital is greatly needed. Thousands of people are getting no medical attention." I had to write, telling her that, much as I would love to help, I couldn't possibly do so because I was so involved with raising money for the school at Tongo. I just couldn't get involved in two fund-raising projects at the same time. I felt so disappointed about having to decline the help she wanted from me. I knew she would be equally disappointed when she got my letter, which had been posted about three months before I arrived in India for the second time.

When I arrived at Ranchi to be met by Sister Bernadette, she told me immediately that in two days' time the ambulance would be taking me to Gotra, where the planned hospital site was. I could see she was quite excited about my arrival and I think she had convinced herself I would help. I remember asking her if she had received my letter. She said no straight away. Of course, in that letter I'd declined to help. I just hadn't got the heart to tell her there, so I allowed myself to be talked into going to Gotra. On the Saturday the ambulance left Tongo very early in the morning to go there. With me were Sister Vianney and Albina. Sister Bernadette would be making her own way from Dorma to Gotra that day and would meet me there.

Just before I returned to India I received a letter from

Dr Irene Tete, Sister Bernadette's sister-in-law, informing me that she and her husband, also a doctor and serving in the Indian army, would eventually be returning to Gotra to supervise the building of this new hospital. But, she said, her husband would not be getting his release date from the army until February and neither of them would be able to meet me at Gotra. Her husband, Sister Bernadette's brother, held a very senior position as a medical officer. Both he and his wife evidently shared this dream of a hospital. "We will work until our last days to build it," she wrote. In her letter she went on to explain that this medical centre would serve a population of 700,000 in the subdivisional area of Simdega, 90 per cent of them tribal people spread among 1,000 villages in this very remote part of India. At present the nearest hospital is at Ranchi, 50 miles away. Many of these tribal people won't even be able to afford the bus ride, let alone the medical treatment once they get there. Consequently, hundreds are dying in an area infested with malaria, dysentery, tuberculosis and countless other diseases. "Every time my husband and I come home to Gotra we find many people have died through lack of proper medical facilities," Dr Tete had written. She explained that her husband had acquired eight acres of land from his own savings to build the new medical centre. On receiving the letter I knew there would be pressure on me to help with this project when I arrived at Gotra, but how on earth was I going to help to raise £100,000 just to make a start with the hospital? They would be expecting a lot of me. I would have to be strong and tell the people of Gotra that I just couldn't help. I also realised that Sister Bernadette was expecting an awful lot from me. If only she'd received my letter telling her I couldn't possibly get involved. But she hadn't and I had a feeling that quite a welcome was being prepared for me in that village.

The ambulance finally arrived in Gotra after a journey

of over five hours. The roads hadn't improved at all. If anything they were worse. The distance was only about 30 miles, but poor roads make any journey in Bihar seem long. I was quite exhausted by the time we arrived. I remember thinking about those smooth roads in England and about how we take so much for granted. On approaching the village down the narrowest of country lanes I thought I could hear music, and sure enough the whole village seemed to have turned out to greet me. The population was probably about 1,000 and hundreds of tribal people were forming a column for this white man from England, this man who they thought would build them their hospital. As the ambulance arrived at the centre of the village I stepped off it to be greeted by Sister Bernadette and other local dignitaries and to be repeatedly garlanded with flowers. I was being pushed from all sides as these excitable people couldn't get near enough to me. The children started singing, trumpets blew, drums were banged and men and women performed tribal dancing. This really was a hero's welcome. How could I get out of this one, I was thinking. I was in an embarrassing predicament. A meal had been arranged for me and I was ushered into what passed for the village hall. Even during the meal the festivities continued. I was in a most awkward situation, probably one of the worst I have ever been trapped in. I was being treated literally like some Indian god.

After a meal I was taken to the planned site just outside the village. The eight acres of land had been marked out for my benefit. I was standing next to Sister Bernadette and finally I told her she mustn't rely on me to raise the necessary money. My letter would have explained all this, I remember saying. If only she had received that letter. I realised I was not only letting her down, but the whole village and thousands throughout Simdega district. They really had expected too much of me. If only I could win the Lottery, then I really could help. What a wonderful hospital could be built on that eight acres, I was thinking while standing in that field. Here I was in a poor tribal area of India praying for a miracle. These desperately poor people who owned absolutely nothing were looking for that miracle and I was unable to give it to them.

As I sit at home writing this chapter I recall the unbelievable poverty I saw during my brief stay in India and think of this world of ours. Why is it that it's such a good life for some, me included, while nearly a third of the world lives in misery, well below the poverty line? Why is it that show business celebrities, including film stars and pop idols, seem to earn so much money that they literally do not know how to spend it? Among the very top earners in England these days are sportsmen, including golfers, boxers and footballers to name but a few. Is Nick Faldo really worth his millions? Did Frank Bruno really earn his fortune when he was knocked out by Mike Tyson in three rounds and was Alan Shearer really worth the £15 million transfer fee that Newcastle United paid for him? He is already a millionaire several times over. My answer to all these questions is an emphatic no. Of course they are not worth that sort of money. Is anybody, for that matter? There is a lot of greed in sport today, particularly the top footballers in English football, who will often hold their clubs to ransom, with their exorbitant wage demands. You will read of a footabller in the last chapter of this book who was a hero of mine, but because he played in a different era, he earned a pittance in comparison to today's super-stars. Yet for me he had twice as much talent. It is reported that Shearer's wages are £30,000 per week. Just think what one week of his pay could do for the village of Gotra - what a start for that new hospital. Let me say that I'm sure those three famous sportsmen are very generous and charitable people, as are a host of show business stars who help the under-privileged of this world. Standing in that tribal part of Simdega district that day I wanted a miracle and I knew God gave us this world for the wealth to be distributed far more equally than it is today.

As I said goodbye to Gotra I left with a sad heart. The village gave me a rapturous sendoff. I felt I'd let Sister Bernadette down terribly. What was I to do? I had to be honest. If only, I kept saying to myself, if only I could help. We then proceeded in the ambulance to the Samtoli convent school, in a village near Gotra, where I was hoping to meet Sister Angela once again. I had met this Ursuline sister at Tongo five years earlier and she had been transferred to Samtoli two years ago. I was anxious to meet her again. On arrival I was met by the principal, Sister Bindu, who was utterly charming. On being taken round the school by her, I only had to look at the children to see the happiness there. More than 2,000 children attend this school. Perhaps the reason why children seem so happy at these convent schools is that they can't believe their luck that they are attending school at all. Thousands and thousands never get the chance, so the ones who do attend are the lucky ones. When I first sponsored Albina through the charity ActionAid, enabling her to have an education, hundreds of other children throughout Bihar were also being sponsored. Then, a few years ago, ActionAid pulled out of Bihar and went elsewhere in India. This was dreadful news for the convent schools of Bihar. Much-needed revenue, which sponsorship brought to the schools, stopped coming in and the move also meant fewer children would be getting an education. It would be wonderful if ActionAid could return to Bihar and sponsor even more children.

On inquiring about Sister Angela I was told she had been the one chosen from Samtoli convent school to take part in the hunger strike at Patna, so unfortunately I would not be meeting the elegant Sister Angela again. After saying goodbye to Sister Bindu and her staff we made our way back to Tongo in the ambulance, but before that I saw a game of cricket being played by some youngsters on a rough patch of ground. All kids in India love to play cricket. I walked over to where this game was being played and asked if I could pick up the bat and play a few shots. The idea was that Albina would take some photos of me actually playing cricket in India. I'd retired from cricket three years earlier and it showed. Could I hit that ball? I just couldn't get near it. I was making a fool of myself. I think I did manage to hit one ball. I walked off that piece of land saying to myself that I'd definitely played my last game of cricket.

Only about 10 miles from Tongo there is a retreat for Catholic priests. Evidently students from all over southern Bihar are chosen to attend. It is near the village of Carondabera, which was on our route back to Tongo that day. Sister Vianney was most keen that I see this religious retreat. It was here that three Catholic priests had been murdered just over 12 months earlier. Sister Vianney had written to me about this ghastly incident and of how it had shaken the whole area, Tongo included. Tongo is peaceful and has never experienced such an example of human depravity. I hope it never does. Apparently one of the students at the retreat decided to murder these priests, who were the only ones at the retreat at the time. This student, a Hindu, disliked Christians intensely. He hated them. One evening he must have gone berserk and in a savage but cold and calculating way he set about murdering the priests. The Ursuline sisters at Tongo knew them personally and were deeply upset. Sister Vianney took me into the actual rooms where the priests had met their deaths. Three rooms, three murders. It was an eerie experience. I could not begin to explain how I felt as I was shown around that retreat. I remember feeling a strange sensation and noticing how cold those rooms were. What didn't help were the large colour photographs of a quite barbaric nature taken of the priests in death, which were in that building. They were the most upsetting photos it has ever been my misfortune to see. The faces were unrecognisable, ears and noses cut off and lying in pools of blood. I had to get out of that building. It had upset me so much. I was then taken to what I can only describe as a shrine, a place of worship where the priests are buried. I came away from that retreat in a sombre frame of mind, contemplating how horrific man's inhumanity to man can be. A few months after the murders a student at Ranchi was beaten quite savagely to death by a large crowd of his fellow students. No one has ever been arrested and nor are they likely to be, because it is widely known that it was this student who committed those despicable murders.

That evening at the dining table the sisters started talking about the hunger strike and whether it was having any effect. They were obviously concerned for all the Ursuline sisters camped outside the chief minister of Bihar's home at Patna. None of them would be eating, including Sister Sarita from Tongo. The chief government minister's name was mentioned again. He certainly was not flavour of the month. When Sister Vianney had written, telling me of the strike, I wrote back saying that when I came to India I could go and see the chief minister myself. I was so concerned for the sisters, that they of all people should have to go on hunger strike. I thought he might just listen to me. I'd got nothing to lose. At this time, while sitting there with them, I had them on quite wickedly.

"This government minister of Bihar - can I go and see him at Patna? He might listen to me," I said.

"He will listen to no one. He is very obstinate," said a sister.

"You say he has broken his leg. I want to see him so I can break his other leg. He deserves it," I replied. Everyone went quiet. Sister Vianney, who always sat beside me at that dinner table, looked as though she couldn't believe her ears. There was also the flicker of a smile. Being a nun, she, like the other sisters, would of course be against any form of violence. But according to the sisters, the minister had no heart. Revenge is sometimes sweet and here was a golden opportunity to punish him.

"Please," I continued with a straight face, "let me break his other leg." I swear that the look Sister Vianney gave me was really four different looks all at one. This is what I saw. First look - yes, please break his leg. Second look - you wouldn't, though, would you? Third look - how could you do such a thing? Fourth look - please, God, forgive me. I don't mean any harm to come to the chief minister. I smiled to myself. I really did believe for a few fleeting seconds that the sisters, particularly Sister Vianney, thought I was prepared to go to Patna, over 100 miles from Tongo, to break the minister's leg. What relief there was when they realised I didn't mean it.

Chapter Five

The Heart Of India

Imagine the scene. Here I was once again in Albina Kujur's home. I'd been invited to spend the day with her family. I was once more in the India of Mahatma Gandhi, the man who so loved the countryside and who had preached peace but died so violently. I was right in the heart of the countryside. More than three quarters of India's population lives in villages and the core business of village India is agriculture. Gandhi felt that the real India was in the countryside, and here I was being feted by village people. I'd received a wonderfully warm welcome amid much singing, dancing and laughing and the rice beer was flowing. I'd been taken to the now familiar table and chair where I'd sat before. Inside that hut a scene from five years ago was about to be recreated. A special meal had been cooked in my honour by Albina's mother. As I looked at the food put before me I couldn't help but think what I'd thought before. These peasant people from the tribe of Oron were known as the original rat eaters of India because they were so poor that they had to eat rats to survive. I also cast my mind back to all my talks and slide shows. I'd told all those different groups of people that I might well have eaten rat's meat. What laughter that had caused. And here I was again wondering about the meat I was about to eat. I could so vividly remember the last time. I'd been told I must eat my meal, otherwise I would offend Albina's mother and all her family and friends. I remember how I forced down whatever it was, all the time thinking I was about to be sick. So what was I to do this time? I could sense many eyes watching this white man's every move. At that moment Sister Terisita, one of the three sisters from the school who had come with me that day, actually put a knife and fork in my hands. I had been politely told to get on with it.

Rice beer came to my rescue. As I'd had several glasses of this so-called beer, it had given me a sort of Dutch courage. Rice beer, incidentally, tastes very much like wine. When last in that hut I'd tried it, but it had done nothing for me. These peasant people seem to thrive on it, though. This time the taste was different and I'd begun to enjoy it. Talk about washing the meal down. I did just that - it was the only way I was going to eat it. There must have been 50 people in that hut that day. Enjoying herself the most was Albina's mother - quite a character, I can assure you. She certainly liked her rice beer and she was quite merry. This lady had hardly left my side. Just like the last time, she was in tears as she greeted me. This peasant farmer's wife, who had given birth to six children, had worked with her husband from dawn to dusk under a blazing hot sun in the fields. Born into this life, she would have known nothing else. Her life on that plot of land behind her home consisted of sowing, transplanting, weeding and harvesting. Albina had told me her mother hadn't been well. She looked so frail and thin, hardly weighing six stone. Her skin was burnt and withered from years of sun exposure. Her life, like that of millions of other women in rural India, had been one of extreme hardship. On that particular day, she was determined to enjoy herself and I for one was not going to stop her. At one stage Albina told her mother to quieten down and go for a short lie down. Albina told me this after speaking to her mother in Hindi. I then jokingly asked Albina to ask her mother if I could lie down with her. When her mother got this message she laughed so much that I thought the roof of the hut would come off. She pointed her fingers at me and herself as if to say "you and me to lie down?" She couldn't believe what I'd said to her. Being deeply religious, the only person she would ever have laid down with in her whole life would have been her husband. This sweet little lady had had an unbelievingly hard life. Going about our comfortable lives in England, we only read of such poverty. If she had had one too many, well, she deserved it. She had earned it and I for one was only too pleased to be with her again.

Indian women love jewellery, however poor they are. I'm sure they would deny themselves literally anything in order to wear their rings, jewellery, necklaces and bangles. Even families who are nearly destitute will buy jewellery as an investment for that terrible day when it has to be sold to avoid starvation. I can imagine the scene when a village girl marries. If and when Albina marries, that home of her parents will be a scene of great celebration. Wedding celebrations can go on for days. Amid the noise of singing, dancing and banging drums she would be covered with jewellery and wearing the most beautiful sari imaginable. She would also be heavily made up, with rings through the nose and goodness knows where. Some brides meet their husbands for the fist time on their wedding day. Indians are fond of saying that love usually comes after marriage rather than before. Most marriages are arranged. It's a father's responsibility to marry his daughter as quickly as possible. Even when a girl is very young her partner may have been picked. It's not uncommon for a 12-year-old girl to marry a man of 60. The girl's father must also save for a dowry. Marrying his daughter off into another family will usually entail a cost in rupees, but sometimes a bullock will be given to the bridegroom's parents. A bullock is priceless in the countryside. Having several daughters can not only be expensive for a peasant farmer but also embarrassing. If he can't get his daughter married off he is stuck with her. But sons are different. Parents are never prouder than when a son is born. As he grows up he farms his father's land as his father grows older. Upon marrying, he will move his new bride into his parents' home and she will become very much part of the family, knowing that one of her main responsibilities is to look after her husband's parents. If a father in the Indian countryside has lots of sons he is indeed a very lucky man.

That day in Albina's home, and it was only a small wooden hut, I'd been with the Bihar Beauties, some only recently married themselves. If these marriages are arranged, the parents are to be congratulated. These young girls, some with babies strapped on their backs, couldn't have looked happier. Marriage obviously suits them. In the countryside it is a sacred institution. In the West marriages are breaking down and, if I am correct, one in three marriages in England today ends in divorce. In India, marriages usually last and partners are committed to each other. If a young mother splits up with her husband in the countryside of India she has nowhere to go. Her parents would certainly not want her back. That would bring shame on the family. There are no social security payments either. With no money, she is destitute. So, no matter how bad a relationship is, a couple will usually stay together. What is most important to these country peasants is their Catholic religion. Before going to Albina's home that day I'd been to the 9 o'clock morning mass at the church in Tongo with Sister Vianney. There were 300 people there that morning. Among them were many young mothers dressed in rags, holding their babies. They had, in all probability, walked miles to come to church. I thought 300 was a good congregation, only for Sister Vianney to tell me that more than 800 people had attended the 5am mass that day. I was also told that the 6am, 7am and 8am services had been well attended, too. God seems to play a big part in these people's lives. They rely very much on the monsoon. They pray for rain, because without it their crops will not grow. When the rain does finally come it can prompt much dancing around the little mud huts. Without the rain nothing grows. Next comes starvation. They pray continually all year round for the fruits of a good harvest. When the crops are gathered in, everyone's happy. At least they have food for the months ahead. Theirs is such a simple life, yet in Albina's home I'd found great happiness. Why is it that the poor people of the world attend church is great numbers, while in the West the opposite often applies? Children are brought up very much in the Christian way. One evening I'd asked Sister Alphonsa why the children at Tongo school were so happy, even though they were born into appalling poverty.

"Mr Brian, they have found God. There's no other explanation for it," she said.

The Bihar Beauties are the beautiful girls from deepest Bihar. I don't think I've ever seen as many lovely-looking young girls as there were in Albina's home that day. Women are generally second-class citizens in India. Some are exploited dreadfully. Their place is very much in the home, obeying their husbands, working the fields and producing children, hopefully sons. Being dutiful wives, they are completely controlled by their husbands. They are also very shy and reserved and certainly not vain, however beautiful they may be. It's accepted that women work harder than men, often doing the real heavy jobs. But what they do like is their singing and dancing. I must say that the tribal dancing I saw in full swing here is totally different to any dancing seen in England. Albina was very much a part of it. I also noticed the vivacious Victoria, Albina's best friend. Now married, she had her baby strapped to her back. Her movements were majestic. Here was the Ava Gardner of the Indian countryside. This black beauty had stunning looks. I shall have to be careful calling her black, otherwise Diane Abbott, the well-known coloured Labour

MP, might call me a racist. To me, black is beautiful just as much as white, and a racist I most certainly am not. I'd hardly be helping India if I were. In the Tongo area, the locals wouldn't know what racism is. Victoria was undoubtedly one of the outstanding Bihar Beauties among many lovely-looking women and girls that day. Victoria has obviously found love in her marriage. One could see how proud her husband was of her by the looks he gave her. It might have been an arranged marriage, but all I could see was love. The real beauty of these Indian country folk is the beauty within. These people from the tribe of Oron are the beautiful people of India and it was my very great pleasure to be with them again.

While in that hut of happiness that day I'd hardly noticed Albina's father. He had also been ill. The hard life he had led had finally caught up with him. His heart is not good and he struggles for breath. He really had altered beyond recognition. His poor body had taken a terrible beating over the years and he was also extremely thin. One just does not find elderly people in India. The average life expectancy is 46. Albina had told me that when her father married her mother it was his third marriage. His two previous wives had died young. As there are so few medical centres in the country areas, early death is a regular occurrence. Malnutrition caused by a simple lack of food is easily the number one cause of death in India today.

After several hours of singing, dancing and drinking (though I must say that though they were in high spirits, not everyone was drinking) I was taken on a tour of the village. People were standing outside their little mud huts, inviting me in. The poverty I saw there reminded me of what I'd seen in the City of Joy in Calcutta. Each hut seemed to have a table, a couple of chairs and a bed. There was always a wooden cross or a picture of Jesus

Christ on the wall. Although these poor peasant people have a dreadfully hard life, I feel that life is probably better for the poor in the countryside than the cities. There are no beggars in the countryside like there are in the big cities. Sometimes one cannot move in the cities for being pestered by beggars. In the countryside most people are working. Virtually all the men are farmers and however poor they are they manage to scrape a living. If they have a bumper harvest that gives them more than enough food from their little plots of land, they will try to sell their crops at a market that could be 20 miles away. Their only means of getting there would be on foot. Pulling a cart full of rice or potatoes to those markets would be extremely hard, but that's their life and they know no other.

In the area around Tongo there are many forests and the huts I visited would be only about half a mile from one of them. If the rats from those forests visit Tongo school then it's absolutely certain they would be scurrying around those huts at night time, too. Just think of the disease they would bring with them. Every hut has its little plot of land to the rear. The poor farmer never owns his hut or land but rents it from some unscrupulous landlord, who charges excessively. If the farmer wants to extend his little plot by renting further land, he commits himself to the landlord for life. Once in debt he remains in debt. When a son takes over the land from his father he will be saddled with the debt too. He will be well and truly tied to the landlord for the rest of his life. This is the way the landlord likes it. He has the farmer in his pocket. Some landlords are extremely rich. They are from either the upper or middle castes and have profited from the poor all their lives. We might think we have fat cats in British industry today, but the fat cats in the Indian countryside are profiting enormously from their excessive rents. Whatever the tenant makes, the landlord takes a good three-quarters of it. He grants the tenant just about enough to live on. There are certainly no luxuries of any kind and if the poor tenant gets into difficulties and can't pay his rent he will, in all probability, be thrown off the land. When that happens he is, of course, finished. He might even end up in one of the big cities begging on the streets. He would still have a family to support. No wonder Mahatma Gandhi wanted to change the injustice of the caste system. He disliked it intensely. In today's India the fat cats are making a fortune through exploitation and corruption on a massive scale. Corruption is everywhere and it's the poor who suffer. India's poor have always suffered. The people I'd been with in Albina's village that day might well have been exploited by some greedy land-lord themselves. Until the caste system is demolished India's poor will always be exploited.

When one thinks of India one automatically thinks of a Third World country out in the subcontinent. We also think of the most appalling poverty imaginable, with thousands of undernourished people dying every day. I feel that to a certain extent I've lived with the poor. I've certainly mixed with them and I feel I also know what they're up against. The poor peasant farmer doesn't ask for much, just to be able to get on with his life. If he is exploited by his landlord he has to accept it. There's simply nothing he can do. I feel I've been to the heart of India, the very soul of it, and I might add it's where my heart is. The world of these people is so different to mine, these people who follow time-tested methods of growing wheat, rice, lentils, vegetables and fruits, these people who live near forests where wild animals roam. The Indian tiger is definitely there, among other animals. Even lions are known to be in those forests. These villagers need to be on their guard at night time, as animals come out of the forests and into the villages looking for food. Occasionally an animal is caught by old-fashioned methods, such as trapping in nets. As the villagers don't own guns, spears are invariably used to kill the animal. Then the village erupts and it's time for another celebration and a feast. That's life today, then, for the people of the tribe of Oron in deepest Bihar, and it's just as it would have been many centuries ago.

Chapter Six

A Cry For Help

On the Monday I saw Albina off on a bus for her trip back to Bihar Sharif. I would see her next on the Saturday, when I would be flying from Ranchi on the first leg of my journey home. She had said she definitely intended to come to Ranchi to say goodbye. She had managed to get a few days off from the school to come and meet me at the airport and be with me as much as possible at Tongo. When not staying with her parents, she would stay at the Tongo school, so I had seen quite a lot of her. I still can't get over the fact that she is a school teacher. What she has achieved is absolutely marvellous. She had studied for her profession at the training college in Lohardaga. At the end of the third year she had failed her final exam. She was so disappointed when she wrote to me of it. She felt she had not only let herself down but also her parents and me as well. Passing those exams was everything to her. She had sacrificed so much. If it hadn't been for her parents she wouldn't have gone to college. I'm sure her parents could have done with her in the fields over the years because many children work long hours in those fields with their families. She had also escaped the arranged marriage situation. Her parents doubtless had many opportunities over the years to marry her off, and of course there would have been no college if they had. But no, they kept her at school until she was nearly 19 and eventually she got to college, and after allowing her to stay there another year in order to pass those exams she did so with flying colours. I was over the moon when she wrote to me with the news. She was a qualified teacher at last and six months later she applied for a position at Bihar

Sharif and got it. When she boarded that bus for Ranchi I was so disappointed not to be going with her, but the sisters were adamant that I shouldn't go and I had to heed their advice.

The multicoloured bus pulled up outside the school gates - Indian buses are painted in the most dazzling colours imaginable and crowded with people, but this one was exceptional. It was overspilling. Ever seen pictures on TV of crowds of people hanging out of bus doors? Well, that was the case here. Packed in like sardines, they were. There must have been dozens sitting on top of this single-decker bus. It really was grossly overcrowded. I didn't think there would be room for Albina, but somehow she managed to get in. It's as though however many people there are waiting at bus stops, they just seem to climb on the bus. They would sit on the bonnet if they could. I saw Albina push her way through and I could just about see her face as the bus sped away. Indian buses really are death-traps. I'd seen nothing like the spectacle of this bus as it moved off to Ranchi. As it picked up speed it was obviously going too fast, swaying and rocking from side to side. It seemed to disappear down the country lanes in no time. How on earth those sitting on top managed to stay on I'll never know. Those roads really are deplorable. If that bus had swayed any more I'm sure a good half of its passengers would have been killed. I thought of Albina and worried for her, but no doubt she would have accepted the conditions without a moment's thought of danger. She is so small and frail and not one person would have given her a seat. Here again it's worth noting the lack of courtesy she would receive as a woman. She would have been pushed from pillar to post. It's no exaggeration to say that each year in India hundreds of buses and lorries finish up in ditches, sometimes completely turned over, and there are many deaths and serious injuries as a result. While on that long journey down to Gotra I noticed three lorries that had ended up in ditches.

Just before leaving for India I had read that buses were continually being blown up. Bombs are apparently being planted under them by terrorists. It seems to be the new way of killing people. At least six buses had been blown up in this way in the last month, with dozens of people blown to bits, so going anywhere by bus in India is a dangerous business. Albina would be on that bus for about two hours on the trip to Ranchi before changing to another bus for an eight-hour journey to Bihar Sharif. I'm sure she would have been exhausted by the time she arrived, but until something is done to repair those dreadful roads, accidents will continue to happen. Also, I'd noticed the words "good luck" in large capital letters on the front of buses and big, heavy lorries. This is a warning for any other vehicles or people who just happen to be in the way. It means "steer clear of me or I will hit you. Stay in the way at your peril." Those words could be seen as a clear message of this sort, but in reality they mean "bad luck." If it's your bad luck to be in the way of those buses or lorries, you will need good luck to survive. On those country roads in Bihar you can hear a big lorry half a mile away, often picking up the noise before you see the vehicle. The horn is constantly blowing, so by the time the lorry or bus appears all smaller vehicles and any people are out of the way. You can really do with any luck going if you haven't moved off the road.

Later that day, Sister Vianney and Sister Alphonsa took me to see families in Tongo village who are suffering real hardship. I know that in this book I have described these Tongo people as the beautiful people of India, which the majority are. Most of these peasant farmers and their wives are in a loving relationship with each other and with their children too, but there are exceptions of the sort one would come across in most parts of the world. We visited the home of one young mother, whose husband had recently left her. She was at her wits' end as to how she was going to manage with her four children, all of them under five. She was getting no help from anyone and with no money coming in she was desperate. There was even the possibility she might have to give her children up for adoption. In another hut we visited we found a wife doing the family washing by the traditional method of slapping wet clothes on stones - extremely hard work. She was working herself to the bone. She had a large family and would also be working in the fields. Her husband, Sister Vianney told me, was lazy and didn't help his wife at all, and, sure enough, there he was stone drunk on rice beer and sleeping it off on waste ground by the hut. I was told that as rice beer costs virtually nothing to make, many men turn to drink. It's a regular thing to see men drunk during the day. The sisters took me to other huts where there was terrible hardship. I know all people are poor in the countryside of India, but the families I was being taken to see really were the poorest of the poor.

Now a word about a cry for help, one which affected me deeply. Sister Alphonsa had told me of one particular case which I found most distressing. As we approached a hut I was told that two little sisters aged seven and six had been abandoned by their parents and were living on their own, all alone in a filthy hut to fend for themselves. The older girl's name was Shashi and the younger one was called Nina. Living next door was a cruel uncle who beat them regularly. The girls' father had left home for another woman about a year ago, leaving his wife and six children. Three of the older children had moved out to be looked after by relatives, leaving the wife with her two little girls and a baby boy of nine months. This woman, said the Ursuline sisters, was a bad woman. She would get drunk on rice beer and also beat her daughters. She had many men friends. One day a lorry driver called at Tongo and slept with her. Having no love for her daughters, the mother just upped and left with the lorry driver to live in Ranchi, taking her baby with her and leaving her two little daughters to survive somehow on their own.

"Please come and see these two little girls. It really is a sad case," said Sister Vianney.

What happened next really did touch my nervous system. As we approached this hut a little girl was wandering around outside looking lost. Sister Vianney asked her where her younger sister was to be told that she had gone with one of her older brothers to Ranchi to try to find their mother. It would be like looking for a needle in a haystack. Sister Alphonsa then took this girl's hand and the three of us followed her into a very filthy hut. Amid the filth I managed to find a wooden box to sit on and sat the girl on my knee. Sister Vianney asked her why she wasn't at school. All she did was shake her head. She was clearly upset and nearly in tears. The girl was in a shocking state, her thin little body a pathetic sight, with legs like matchsticks. She was as light as a feather. It was as though I was holding a baby. At this point the cruel uncle I'd been told about came in. He didn't say a word and sat on another wooden box facing me just two yards away. He directed his gaze at me while smoking a cigarette. How he'd got money to pay for cigarettes I'll never know - probably from the small amount his wife earned by slaving away in the fields. As soon as that man walked into the hut I could sense the little girl was frightened of him. She was shaking with fear. The man's eyes never left me. He was on the small side, but well built and he might have been trying to intimidate me.

All this time the sisters and I were speaking in English, so the man wouldn't know what we were talking about. The sisters told me Shashi was not going to school because her uncle wouldn't let her go. She looked to be in need of a good meal and I asked the sisters if I could give her some money so that she might at least buy some food. They told me that under no circumstances was I to give her money because her uncle would only knock her about the moment we were gone and take it from her. Now I don't mind saying that I think I'm as placid as the next man, but sometimes there's a different me. My wife will tell you I can lose my cool on occasion, and this was one of those occasions. I was seething inside at this bully of an uncle. Here I was with this slip of a girl, just seven years of age, and she was shaking like a leaf. She looked terrified of her uncle and was obviously in a very distressed state. He still watched my every move and certainly resented me being in that hut. He was, I'm sure, waiting for me to give him some rupees. This I was definitely not prepared to do. After a few minutes the sisters got up to leave. I put Shashi down and walked out of the hut. I'd shown compassion to this girl but left her to this man. It made my blood boil that he was mistreating her, this tiny mite, and her sister. If there's one thing in this world that really gets my back up and fills me with revulsion, it's the thought of children being battered or abused. Who knows, maybe the girl was being sexually abused. It upset me considerably as I walked away from that hut. Twenty yards later, I turned round and there was Shashi staring at me, a stare that seemed to say "don't leave me", a stare that seemed to say "please help me", a stare that filled me with such guilt that I was leaving her to this man. Did this girl ever smile, I asked myself. Even 100 yards away from that hut I turned round again and there she was, neither smiling nor waving and looking so tiny in the distance. As I walked away from Shashi with the two sisters I had the feeling that they had deliberately taken me to meet her and her sister in the hope that I might help in some way. What I do know is that I couldn't get that little girl out of my mind.

In my bedroom that evening, waiting for the clanging of the bell that summoned me to the evening meal, I thought of the dreaded uncle and it disturbed me. I could quite easily have knocked him off that box he was sitting on, although of course that would have proved nothing, as I was giving him 30 years and would be no match for him. Here I was being confronted with two little girls who were being subjected to regular beatings, and perhaps something even worse. I know a lot of this is going on in England these days. Paedophiles are destroying children's lives. We all read these horror stories in our newspapers every week. In all my 29 years as an insurance man, where my job involved going into people's homes, I can honestly say I never saw a child with a black eye or any other injury inflicted by human hand, or for that matter any signs of the timid behaviour that hints at violence in the home. They may well have been beaten or abused, but I was never aware of it. I'm sure, though, that had I come across it I would have taken the necessary action. I would certainly have reported it, but thankfully I never did come across it. So what was I to do in this tragic situation of an Indian girl not far from death's door? In England I could at least have done something about it, but I was in India, a foreign country. It was nothing to do with me, but I had to act. I just had to rescue her from that living hell. I kept thinking of her all alone in the dark at night with her uncle next door, one timid little girl, frightened and whimpering. I'd found a girl who couldn't smile. Did she know what it was to laugh? She had been deserted by both parents and must spend many hours crying. All these thoughts were going through my head as those deep staring eyes haunted me. I just had to act, but how was I to do so?

At the dinner table I raised the subject of the child I'd

seen. Most sisters knew of the mother. She was certainly well known and had a reputation for having had many affairs. The Ursuline sisters do not mince their words and repeated what I'd heard earlier in the day, namely that the mother was a bad woman. I asked what could be done to help the child and I was told she would continue to be beaten up. Now at this Tongo school there are 400 boarders. All of them are orphans, who would have been taken in by the sisters over the years to live at the school and live there permanently because, with no parents or relations to look after them, they wouldn't otherwise survive. These boarders are so well looked after by the sisters and the rest of the staff at Tongo that their happiness is an absolute joy to see. Why, therefore, couldn't Shashi and her younger sister Nina become boarders at the school. Here was a golden opportunity for them to be taken from their home. Surely here was a deserving case of two little girls being subjected to appalling abuse. I had no real evidence of sexual abuse, but there was definite physical abuse. I was then told by the sisters that only children with nowhere to go are taken in as boarders. They appreciated that Shashi and her sister lived in dreadful fear of their uncle and they dearly wanted to help, but, they said, at least the girls had a roof over their heads.

"For a child to come here it really must be a deserving case. The child must definitely be an orphan, and that means that there are not only no parents to look after them, but no relations either. At least those two little girls have a home to live in, however awful it might be," said Sister Michael.

"The only way those two girls could become boarders would be if someone paid for them to attend," said Sister Alphonsa. The ball was being put in my court. Two terrified little kids in India wanted my help. How could I possibly not help them? I wanted those girls away from that filthy hut. I was still boiling with rage inside, but trying to stay calm. But the memory of that little girl, sat on my knee and unable to stop shaking, compelled me to act. I just knew that if it was at all humanly possible I had to help. I wanted them out of the reach of this uncle who was inflicting such harm on them. I'd got to beat the bully so there would be no more abuse, and I particularly wanted to see one little girl smiling again.

The City Centre (early morning), the good part of Calcutta

The poor part of Calcutta

The author (in cap) in the slums of Calcutta, known as The City of Joy

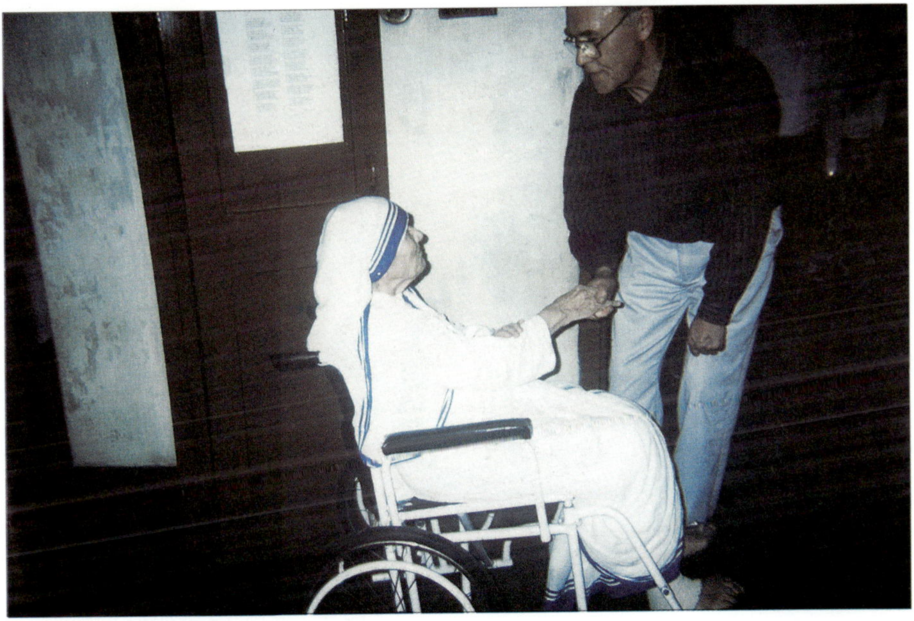

A Red Letter Day. The Author meets Mother Teresa for the second time.
In five years he had noticed a marked deterioration in her health

Inside Mother Teresa's orphanage

What a welcome at Ranchi Airport. The author with Albina and friends

The Town Centre of Ranchi

The country roads are dangerous, as demonstrated here by the not-infrequent sight of a lorry in a ditch

Women working on road repairs in the countryside of Bihar

The author with Albina at the welcome party in her parents home. His wife, on seeing this photograph, remarked how much her husband had aged while in India

Albina and Victoria

Two of the Bihar beauties with their babies at the welcome party

More of the Bihar beauties

The new school building

Tongo schoolchildren gather for the official opening of the new school building, with six new classrooms

Tongo schoolchildren singing and dancing at the opening of this new school building

The schoolchildren in their new classroom

The completed school wall

The main entrance of the Ursuline Tongo convent school, with the new gates

The Tongo village Catholic Church is situated in the school grounds

Out of retirement. The author plays cricket again

The author with twelve of the Ursuline sisters of Tongo (The Divine Sisters)

The Divine Sisters with their headscarves.
The author's last evening with them

Alex Young "The Golden Vision" (Everton and Scotland)

Chapter Seven

Bihar Babies

Sister Frederic's dispensary is a special place, which I visited one morning. She sees to the needs of all 1,300 children at the school, although one could also say she is the village doctor for the people of Tongo. Sister Frederic herself is a special lady. One could almost call her dispensary a hospital - not that operations are performed there, but there are wards for patients. The illness she deals with most is malnutrition. Sometimes children just do not get enough to eat. The children who come to school do, of course, get regular food, but there are a lot of children who do not attend the school and they are the undernourished ones. Sister Frederic has a pill for every need. Any child who falls ill and finishes up in one of these wards does indeed get the most loving and caring nurse looking after them in the shape of Sister Frederic, a real Florence Nightingale. If I refer rather fondly to Sister Michael as my auntie, then I would see Sister Frederic as my granny. Not that she's all that much older than me, because she's not, but I have very affectionate memories of my grandmother, who was so sweet and kind, and that is exactly what Sister Frederic is. If I was never to have made it back to England because I'd been taken terribly ill at the school, I would gladly have settled for her to look after me. I have great affection for her and I know she has for me. We have a great rapport together - a more caring lady you couldn't wish to meet.

Her dispensary is quite a smart brick building in the school grounds near the front gates, which of course is very handy for all the Tongo villagers who call to see her. This particular morning when I came to see her I fully expected her to be busy. When I was last in Tongo I know she was rushed off her feet. I don't think she gets much help, either. I remember there were children on the wards five years ago with malaria and Sister Frederic feared she might lose them. But this morning she wasn't busy. Not one child was on the wards and because for once she had time on her hands we had quite a chat. Among many other duties, she has of course delivered many babies into the world and because of this there was one question I just had to ask her. It concerned newborn baby girls being killed at birth. There are many midwives in the state of Bihar, probably thousands at a rough guess, but I'd read some shocking things about them in the English press. Apparently midwives were killing baby girls within minutes of birth. I gave Sister Frederic a newspaper cutting I'd brought from England. It was about two years old and described Bihar as India's wild west in more ways than one.

The reason I wanted Sister Frederic to read that article was that I was looking for some answers. Did the killing of baby girls happen in the Tongo area? That newspaper piece told of a midwife, known as a kindly grandmother, who murdered unwanted baby girls at birth, carrying out this gruesome task for 50 rupees - about £1. As I've said previously in this book, baby girls are often less than welcome to a father in the countryside of India and it can bring great crisis to a family if nothing but girls are born to it. A boy, meanwhile, is a gift from God. The peasant farmer prays for a boy, while girls are subjected to many hours of loneliness, often ignored and rarely appreciated as they grow older. They are not valued for their beauty or sweetness of voice and of course the dowry for his daughter's marriage is a constant worry for the struggling farmer, so to spare the embarrassment and many other problems associated with having too many baby girls, some are being murdered. The article went on to explain that the quickest method of killing was for the baby to be strangled with a piece of rope, to be poisoned with fertiliser or to have a lump of black salt put in their throat. Sometimes a baby's spine would be broken by bending it back. These horrendous acts are happening in Bihar today. The grandmother was quoted as saying that in her heart she didn't want to kill the babies, but her family needed the money. When the babies were dead she wrapped them in a piece of cloth and either threw them in the river or buried them in undergrowth, where she knew they would quickly be found by animals and eaten. This elderly midwife, this grandmother, had convinced herself she was carrying out mercy killings because female babies are so unpopular. She also explained in the article that even if baby girls go on to survive birth they are usually denied medicine when they fall ill. They are rarely sent to school and their only use as they grow older is their capacity for manual work.

The Indian authorities deny the existence of female infanticide, but recently social workers from an Indian non-government organisation partly funded by Unicef interviewed 85 Bihar midwives and found the practice to be quite common. Just about all the midwives admitted to killing up to four baby girls per month and all of them carried out the ghastly deed at the request of the father. He usually waited outside his hut and when told his wife had given birth to a girl he would order the midwife to kill the baby. One midwife said that refusing a father's order to kill the baby would see her beaten up. In one case a midwife was shut in a room and told by the father, who already had five daughters, that she would not leave it alive unless the latest newborn baby girl was killed. So she hanged the baby using a small rope. The child took two hours to die on the end of that rope. The mother was hysterical, as she didn't want this to happen. There is no register of births in

Bihar. No one knows officially how many babies are killed. Some midwives say female infanticide is looked on as a form of family planning in some areas. One particular mother had given birth to 12 girls, 10 of whom had been killed. I know that this will provoke condemnation and revulsion from all who read my book in England. We in the West really do live in a different world.

Obviously one must condemn in the strongest possible terms the despicable act of killing a baby. In England and other Western countries it would be viewed as murder, plain and simple. The person tried and convicted for such an act would get life imprisonment, but I would emphasise once again the sheer desperation of people living in the country areas of India, not just Bihar but all over the vast subcontinent. Those midwives, I'm sure, hate themselves for doing what they do. We all have a conscience and no one escapes it. Those midwives are surely no exception. How can they live with it, we may well ask. They must despise themselves for those few rupees that they earn. But, in their defence, that money is often the difference between life and death. Those midwives would have their own families to support and when their children are starving and dying through lack of food is it all that surprising that these dreadful crimes are being committed? All over India people survive from day to day. I believe a person is capable of doing literally anything in order to feed themselves and their children. One must condemn any killing, whatever the motive, but we in the West just do not know how the poor survive below the poverty line. Let us be thankful that we have never been placed in that position ourselves.

Later that day Sister Frederic gave me back the newspaper cutting. She was visibly shocked. I thought I could see tears in her eyes. Did I really have to upset her with that article? Was I that callous? I felt really sorry for asking her to read it. She told me she could only speak for the Tongo area of Bihar and said that, to her knowledge, there was no killing of baby girls there.

She said: "I know dreadful things happen in certain areas of the state, but babies are definitely not killed at Tongo." I must add here that having visited Tongo twice in the last five years I would have been very shocked indeed if I'd found that babies were being killed there. I'd mixed with these country people, I'd visited their homes, I'd laughed with them and, apart from a few instances - I'm thinking particularly of those two girls who were regularly beaten up by their uncle - I'd found nothing but love. Hadn't I described Albina's family and friends as the beautiful people of India? If there had been any murdering of babies they had concealed it very well. Their happiness was a joy to see and, especially bearing in mind their Catholic religion, I couldn't possibly contemplate any evil of that kind happening. If anyone is to blame, it must be the government of Bihar. There is no doubt that the higher caste officials who run it would not be bothered with the problems of the poor. They know what's going on and do nothing, but nothing surprises me any more about this state. There's so much corruption. I've read such a lot about Bihar in the last five years. It really is the Wild West. When I was there five years ago, the local elections were on. Polling stations were being blown up and people were being told how to vote. Gangsters, really a form of Mafia, have a firm grip on government officials, politicians and police, but Tongo, as I've said before, is peaceful, probably because it is so far off the beaten track. There are certainly no baby girls being killed in Tongo. Judging by the look on Sister Frederic's face I'd really upset her, but I just had to know that what happened in other areas of Bihar didn't happen in Tongo, and, believe me, I was grateful for it.

Before I leave this subject, I have to report that

another form of child murder is being carried out in Bihar today, and what I am about to describe is definitely not for the squeamish. In fact, it's even more disturbing than female infanticide. The mediaeval practice of ritual child sacrifice is rearing its ugly head, not just in Bihar but also in other states. Babies and children are being killed in the belief that the act will bring prosperity from the gods. Infants are being kidnapped by strangers and sacrificed in the name of religion. Hinduism in India runs even deeper than a set of beliefs and customs and it is certainly a way of life for the vast majority of the population. It originated among the Aryan tribes in about 1500BC, when they first arrived in the subcontinent. Worship takes many forms, from private prayer to public festivals. There are more than 330 million gods and goddesses in India and yet all are as one. These gods are worshipped in towns, cities and villages throughout the country and worship centres on the trinity of Brahma (The Creator), Vishnu (The Preserver) and Shiva (the Destroyer). In the Hindu faith, its purpose is to free the soul from worldly existence. All sorts of offerings are made to the gods in order to please them. All that the poor peasant has to offer the gods are his vegetables, which are grown on plots of land throughout India's countryside. If there was a temple in his village he would regularly take a basket of vegetables there, or he might leave them under a banyan tree, all of this done to appease the gods. Other gods or goddesses may only be satisfied with a blood sacrifice, in which blood is spilt in their honour. The average Indian, whether he's a farm worker or a factory worker, constantly wishes for a better life. To achieve it, he must please the gods at all times with certain sacrifices. Failure to make them or to ignore the needs and wishes of the gods is to court disaster, because without the help of the gods, Indians believe, prosperity is not possible.

In the north eastern part of Bihar, where the majority

of its people live (the population of Bihar being 86,374,465 is bigger than many countries) there has been quite a dramatic increase in the kidnapping of babies and children. Evidently, the evil trade is flourishing. Children, when taken, simply vanish off the face of the earth. They are being stolen from their homes to satisfy the gods. Real horror stories are filtering through about these dreadful abductions and what happens to the children when they are sacrificed. Talk about lambs being led to the slaughter. This is certainly what the practice amounts to. I might add that, thank heaven, I have never witnessed any of these ceremonies. How could I possibly witness anything as evil as that? I have contemplated at great length how I would be able to describe how a child is killed in one of these horrific rites. Having written it down in a variety of ways I know I could never feel entirely comfortable with what I'd written. In fact, I've felt quite sick and upset in trying to describe it, so I shall spare the reader from hearing about this most gruesome of practices, which is all in the name of appeasing the goddess Kali. There has probably always been some form of ritual child sacrifice in India. Even though it was outlawed in 1865, this most barbaric variety of child murder is once more becoming part of the way of life of a secret religious sect operating in some Indian states.

What I've written of is the dark side of Hinduism. As with many religions the world over, there are extremes. Often, cults are formed which perform evil practices. In India today there is an old eastern cult carrying out pagan practices, with human beings being the supreme offering and children being especially favoured. It is well-known that animal blood has always been spilt in temples throughout India to please the gods. But the reviving of the practice of killing the young is spreading at an alarming rate among many states. Often this cult plays on the poor and the peasant farmers' families are particularly at risk and most likely to be vulnerable. He has many children and his only income comes from his near-exhausted plot of land. No money can be made from the vegetables he grows because the monsoon was a poor one and nothing much has grown. Having borrowed from a village money lender or some unscrupulous landlord, he's in debt up to his neck. He is at the end of his tether. His family is dying of hunger. At the lowest moment of his life he is approached by this cult, which informs him that giving up one of his children for sacrifice will please the gods. Through doing this he will achieve prosperity and never be poor again. To spill a child's blood is the ultimate sacrifice to the goddess Kali. This deity has three eyes, one in the forehead, and a necklace of human skulls hung around its naked body, which has four arms. In most illustrations, it also seems to have its extra-large tongue hanging out. Kali is the goddess of destruction and, goes the belief, would be well pleased with a child sacrifice. The father, on hearing this, allows one of his young children to be sacrificed and the terrified child is led away, having been told that he or she is the favoured one, specially picked to please Kali. The poor father, on realising the sheer enormity of what he's done, could well commit suicide. But, even more distressing is the kidnapping of children from their homes while their parents are out in the fields. The village people of north Bihar now live in constant fear of their children disappearing. They might just be lucky and, about a week after their child goes missing, its mutilated body is found in a shallow grave, at least allowing them to give it a proper funeral.

Pagan religious rituals are said increasingly to be replacing conventional worship as the number of child disappearances increases. The situation affects all levels of Indian society, as people from all social standings and castes are involved. Politicians have even been arrested in this hideous practice. But more often than not these killings go unchecked. Corruption in high places means some are literally getting away with murder. Helpless and defenceless children are being murdered and the crimes usually go unsolved. The authorities will not acknowledge that human sacrifices exist on such a large scale as they do. Could it be that history is repeating itself and that ritual child sacrifice has returned from the Dark Ages? In one of the states where such ghastly incidents have happened, some villagers have taken the law into their own hands and handed out their own punishment. More than 50 women were accused of witchcraft and were either stoned to death or hanged by neighbours after dozens of children had been kidnapped. When one hears of incidents like that, it really brings the Old Testament to mind.

Please do not believe that such practices are part of everyday Hinduism, because they are not. The perpetrators belong to a cult that merely hides behind Hinduism. There have always been cults and sects who practise evil all over the world and I'm sure there always will be. I happen to love Tongo and in the area around it there are some of the sweetest school children imaginable, and I have a great love for them, too. Not for them the Western way of condoms and the pill at 14, which is what happens to many school girls in today's Britain. No, theirs is a world of innocence, of long ago, the way we were, so to speak, and how the world was when I was a boy growing up. These school children are the innocents of India. Their innocence is not unlike a young flower growing until it reaches full bloom. The innocents of India are being exposed to cruel and wicked practices. Those kids in Tongo are special and what I saw in them was a beautiful innocence of a sort long-since departed from Britain. Theirs is a natural innocence that only children can have, and the thought of ritual child sacrifices being practised in areas near Tongo fills me with such revulsion. The sheer brutality of a little girl being led away to be sacrificed to the gods is hardly bearable for me to even think about. How would I have felt, therefore, if I'd learnt that these evil child sacrifices were being performed at Tongo? I'm pleased to report, though, that as with female infanticide, child sacrifices do not happen there. Not at present, anyway. For the future, however, who knows?

It was around this time during my stay that the hunger strike ended. If anything, the Ursuline sisters of Bihar and the school teachers of all the state's senior schools had scored a resounding victory. The sisters at Tongo were jubilant. Sister Sarita, the representative from Tongo school, had arrived back from Patna on Tuesday evening. In the dining room after the evening meal she gave a very comprehensive report to all the sisters. She started by saying that more than 5,000 teachers, including many Ursuline sisters, had supported the strike. Because of the conviction behind the action, more than 60,000 students had been affected. For three days Sister Sarita and many others had camped outside the chief minister's home in Patna in order to bring about as much disruption to the city as was humanly possible. Belly Street, one of the main roads, had been blocked off by crowds of strikers, causing much confusion. After three days of such disruption, the chief government minister and his administration caved in. The strike had caused dreadful confusion. The chief minister agreed to all the strikers' demands and to give pay back-dated 18 months. The Tongo sisters were thankful the strike had been settled, and I could see they were quite relieved.

Sister Sarita said there had been much rejoicing at Patna. No one involved in the hunger strike had eaten. She and the others hadn't had any food for the three days they were camped outside the chief minister's home. To much laughter, I remarked that now, thankfully, I wouldn't have to go to Patna to break the chief minister's good leg. This was the first time I'd met Sister Sarita and I was most impressed. She is the headmistress of the senior school at Tongo. What impressed me most about her was that it was obvious she would certainly be no pushover. In another life she could have been the trade union official or shop steward. Having been a very minor union official while I was still working, I could have done with Sister Sarita on my side. I'd rather have her with me than against me. She was rightly proud of her achievements.

I wondered if I was seeing some sort of history in the making, because I'd never heard of nuns going on hunger strike before. It was running contrary to their Christian beliefs. Say that strike had gone on and on for many weeks. Say the chief government minister of Bihar had been stubborn and refused to relent. Would those Ursuline sisters really have starved themselves to death outside the minister's home in Patna? Would they really have died for their cause? However justified it was, I tend to think that they wouldn't have. I'm sure common sense would have prevailed, but I know they were very determined. Fortunately it was never put to the test. I only hope the minister keeps his word. He must have felt threatened and vulnerable with so many Ursuline sisters and school teachers camped outside his home. One can say something when cornered because there is no escape, but that minister can now easily change his mind. This is a regular occurrence in India. Promises are made and then broken, so could the sisters trust him? If he breaks his promise to such Christian people who are doing such good in the world, then I for one will be quite angry. I may yet have to go back to India to break that minister's leg. Seriously, though, I really would be annoyed and so disappointed for people I'm so close to and with whom liberties should not be taken. But that evening, Sister Sarita was quite ecstatic.

"Bravo, we have succeeded in our struggle," she said. The victory of course meant the senior school girls would be back at school again the next day. They had been so miserable about not being able to attend classes. The strike had disrupted their school work and there were many smiling faces as they walked through the gates again the next morning.

Chapter Eight

The Divine Sisters

(Women of supreme excellence or worth)

The Ursuline sisters of Bihar, as I've already stated in this book, first came to Ranchi in 1901. They would no doubt have left comfortable Belgian homes for a new life in the outback of India, these four white women whose greatest comfort would be God. They would certainly not have had too many comforts in the wilderness of the countryside of Bihar in those days. The hardships and obstacles they encountered must have been considerable, and at the turn of the century they would definitely have been going into areas where no white person had been before. Having been told about those women by the sisters at Tongo I have the utmost respect for them. What brave women they were. When they arrived in India all those years ago it must have been similar to what the white missionaries discovered in the great continent of Africa at about the same period. No doubt about it, they would be going into some extremely hostile areas, but their great Catholic faith and their love for the Indian school children to whom they were giving an education would be most rewarding. Just imagine a lower-caste child born into a peasant family in 1901. They wouldn't even know what having an education meant. Going to school was just not of their world, and a child's early life would be spent helping parents out in the fields. This is the way it had happened for centuries, but with the arrival of four Ursuline sisters children were at last being given an education.

Finally, children were reaping the benefits of learning, but it wouldn't have been easy convincing parents to let their children attend school. The sisters would have been looked on with great suspicion - after all, the children were wanted in the fields for work. What was this education the sisters were forever talking about? Was it really necessary, the peasant farmer no doubt asked. The sheer bigotry encountered by the sisters from people going through life illiterate would have been immense. Those people would have taken some persuading, but those four white women succeeded in their mission. As the years went by, more schools started opening and more sisters came from Belgium, arriving in the Ranchi and Gumla districts. But the sisters would always be battling against the escalating problem of growing population, which still exists today. There have never been enough schools in India. The population continues to grow at an alarming rate - 20 million a year. Today in India, children are still crying out for an education. How can a Third World country cope with this situation? However many schools are built, it never seems to be enough. It is like trying to fill a bucket with water when it has a large hole in it. In my previous book I tried to make a case for contraception. Until some sort of birth control is used, India's overpopulation problem will remain. India, the world's largest democracy, has enormous problems, something that would have been readily apparent to those Ursuline sisters all those years ago.

Sister Vianney, who is of course one of today's breed of Ursuline sisters, is carrying on the wonderful work that those first four Belgian sisters started in 1901. She, along with 500 other Ursuline nuns in the state of Bihar has given her life to God and to Indian school children. Sister Vianney is one of the Divine Sisters, as I call them. When I was last at Tongo those five years ago, I jokingly called the Ursuline sisters there, the Divine Sisters of Tongo. I make no apology for likening them to some form of supreme human being, because that's exactly what they are. If, as you read this book, it seems as if I put them on a pedestal, then so be it. Without the love and care those sisters gave me while I was with them on my two visits to India I couldn't possibly have enjoyed my stay with them the way I did. I have such a wonderful rapport with them, something I know will stay with me forever. My good friend Sister Vianney was the sister assigned to look after me on my second visit. You will read in this chapter how she washed me, dressed me and massaged my back when I was in great pain. With her permission, I publish a letter she wrote for me when I was in Tongo. I hope the message in it will in some way convey the life of an Ursuline nun.

"I, Sister Vianney, belonging to the congregation of the Ursuline sisters of Tildonk, reside in Tongo. I was born in Kerala in the south of India and was brought up and educated there until the age of 19. I have four sisters and one brother. Three sisters are married and the other two girls (including myself) have joined in religious life. My mother is still alive and my father has gone to Eternal Reward (death). I joined religious life at the age of 19 in 1963 and was sent to an unknown place, entirely different in food, culture and language and far away from home. I struggled to adjust myself to the new place and people, and the disciplinary way of life even tempted me to leave and go home. But an inner calling made me stick to it. In 1966 I made my temporary confession to God and to the congregation of the three vows of chastity, poverty and obedience. Three years later I committed myself to God and to the congregation for life. My congregation, on seeing my talents and interest, sent me for higher studies in science and maths. From 1972 I was engaged in education work, teaching children at Tongo school. At present I am a flourishing member of my congregation and happily serving my beloved through the teaching of children.

"We (the Ursuline sisters) I believe that the congre-

gation of Tildonk, to which we are called as women, is a gift from the Holy Spirit, given to the church for the building of God's kingdom. Anyone who has the call from God can commit herself to the congregation by the three vows, chastity, poverty and obedience. Those who join us are given ample time to know the congregation and to test and understand whether their vocation is genuine or not. After three years the candidate can make a temporary profession, which can be extended to six years. Then the candidate is free to make her final vows or leave the congregation. Even after final, perpetual, vows, one is free to leave with permission of the Superior. No-one can have this life, which is fruitful and joyous, unless she is called by God and has a deep union with Him through fidelity in prayer and discipline of mind and body. This life is a free gift from God, who chooses as his followers very ordinary people with lots of limitations. Generosity and readiness is needed to follow Christ. We may fall, but we get up again and follow Him, who will never leave us.

"The founder of this congregation was Father John Lambertz, who took the charism of St Angela Merici, whose life was profoundly rooted in God. Her wholehearted response to God's infinite love and her deep union with Him gave her a great inner freedom. Throughout her life this freedom led St Angela on one single movement to contemplate God and to serve Him in the church and in the world of her times.

"St. Angela's personal asceticism and simplicity enabled her to make prophetic vision. Her power to discern the particular needs of her times and her spirit of courage and daring impelled her, in obedience to the holy spirit, to establish a company of virgins who would live their consecrated lives in the world. The congregation has become international, found in many countries and approved by the Holy See. Our main charism is proclaiming the

Good News through education - high school, junior school, college and training for women. Besides this there is medical care, social work, work for the uplifting of the poor and awareness of justice and the rights of the illiterate.

"If anyone is inspired to live and do service to Mankind, they are welcome to join the Ursuline congregation of Tildonk."

Sister Vianney.

Sister Vianney is an extremely jolly person. Like all today's Ursuline sisters, bar two remaining Belgian sisters in Bihar, she is Indian by birth. My introduction to her came when she nearly scalded me with hot soup. At the dinner table during what I think was the second night of my first visit to Tongo, she was pouring the soup into my bowl while talking to someone else. All at once the hot soup was being poured into my lap. The heat was so intense that I remember nearly jumping out of my chair. She howled with laughter, along with the other sisters. I could never forget Sister Vianney after that. Whenever my wife and I go out for dinner and soup is being served I am always on edge and might just say to the waitress "don't spill it over me, will you." Little would she know that it did actually happen once. For that reason alone I can never forget Sister Vianney.

An old friend came to see me on the sixth evening of my time spent in Tongo. I was sitting at the dining table with the sisters after dinner when who walked in but Sister Angela. Four days before, as you will recall, I had gone to the village of Gotra to see Sister Bernadette and visited the convent at Samtoli in the hope of seeing Sister Angela, but alas she had been chosen to represent her school at the hunger strike in Patna. On returning from Patna after the strike had been called off, she had been told of my visit. She had caught the first available bus for a four-hour journey to Tongo. It was a lovely surprise as she walked into that dining room. I could hardly get out of my chair to greet her because by then I was already in considerable pain. I was really in agony at times. In fact, the sisters had resorted to putting a hot water bottle at the base of my back at evening meal times. I must have looked a comical figure sitting straight up in a rather big and uncomfortable chair. Amid much laughter, mostly about my back, Sister Angela recalled the problems I had had five years ago. She herself had lost none of her good looks. She certainly hadn't aged. She had played her part along with the other sisters at Patna and was in a buoyant mood now that the strike was over. I then asked her if she would come to my room to continue our conversation, simply because the chair there was more comfortable. She immediately agreed.

"We never did get that walk," I said as we sat talking in my room. We laughed about that because five years ago she had promised to come for a walk with me and we had arranged to meet in the school grounds after classes had finished. But evidently she forgot all about it and that evening I'd asked her where she'd got to. She was very apologetic. I remember thinking I'd been stood up by a nun. "I couldn't have been very important to you," I remember saying, but she had forgotten and promised to walk with me another time. That time was certainly not going to be now. With my back in the state it was in, I couldn't walk anywhere. Anyway, she was returning to Samtoli the next day, so we wouldn't make it. But the reason I wanted to talk to her was to discover why she had become a nun and to find out whether she was happy with her chosen life. She'd be about 40 now. Why had she decided to devote herself to God? I was to ask her some really searching questions, and she answered with the utmost honesty. The conversation went like this:

"You really are quite attractive," I began.

"Yes, I know I am, and thank you," she replied.

"Do you ever feel you have missed out on anything?" I asked.

"What do you mean 'missed out on anything'?" she enquired.

"Well, you could be happily married with children of your own," I said.

"I know that, but I chose my life and I'm very happy," she said.

"But it could have been so different, couldn't it?" I persisted.

"Yes, it could have been quite different, but right from a very early age I wanted to become a nun. I wanted to serve the Catholic church. I wouldn't want to be doing anything other than what I'm doing with my life. My life is serving the Lord, which brings me great happiness. He is my life," said Sister Angela.

"But, with the life you lead, you wouldn't know what it's like to really love someone in the same way as you would know if you had been married," I countered.

"Yes, I accept that but I am sworn to chastity anyway," she responded.

"But sometimes you must think about what you might be missing," I continued.

"You mean sex," came the reply.

"Well, yes," I said with a stammer.

"Look, everyone has feelings of that nature, no matter who they are, and that includes me. But those feelings are quickly put out of my mind. All these sisters at Tongo, or wherever they may be, have these feelings or have had them in the past. We are all human beings, you know - even Ursuline nuns," explained the sister.

"Would the other sisters here all be like you?" I asked.

"Yes, they would all be virgins here, all 16 of them," she replied, adding: "Look, we really are missing nothing in our lives. We chose this life. You have seen the happiness of the sisters here. We love God. He really is our life. We are most proud to serve Him and if it means going without certain things in this life, then so be it."

I must admit I've never seen a happier bunch of women anywhere than the divine sisters. They are not only based in Tongo, but all over Bihar. They really have found God and feel they are missing nothing whatsoever from their lives. They would tell me that God has picked them out to serve Him and that they are the chosen ones. In their prayers, they pray that the rest of the world can be as happy as they are. Having visited them twice, I can vouch for the true happiness of these Ursuline sisters. They own nothing in this life, but what they do have is a type of wealth in this world that we all struggle to find. They really are married to Him. That's why these brides of Christ want for nothing.

The week was going by quickly and in no time it was Wednesday. This particular day it had been decided that I should be taken to Gumla, the town I'd travelled through on the day I'd arrived from Calcutta. I'd wanted to do some shopping for my family, but my worry was whether my back would hold out through all the constant banging up and down that surely lay in wait on some of the worst roads it's ever been my misfortune to travel on. That morning I was in a terrible predicament. Because of my back I was beginning to feel quite useless. I couldn't even bend down or dress myself. Just now my back was at its worst. So who was going to wash and dress me, I wondered. Sister Vianney came to my rescue, giving me a good wash-down. With me only wearing a pair of underpants, she washed my armpits, chest, arms and legs. As none of the showers or baths work at Tongo I was grateful for any help. But I had to smile to myself about this Ursuline nun who was taking such an interest in me. She even hinted that if I wanted washing anywhere else, she would oblige, but I declined her kind invitation. I was not going to let Sister Vianney, who was sworn to chastity, see me in the nude, although it is hardly an unforgettable sight. She did rub some ointment on my back, but she was no Sister Sushila, who had the most caring hands imaginable. She was the nun who had massaged my back during my last stay at the school. Her work done, Sister Vianney dressed me and after breakfast I was taken to the waiting ambulance and placed in the front passenger seat with another hot water bottle on my back. The vehicle then made its way to Gumla, 18 miles away. If I thought I had been in pain already that day, I was going to be in considerably more pain half an hour later.

In the ambulance with me was Sister Scholastica, Sister Michael, Sister Vianney, Sister Alphonsa and Sister Angela, who we would be saying goodbye to at Gumla as she caught a bus to the Samtoli convent school. I did get some comfort from the hot water bottle and the driver was travelling extra slowly because of me, but the sisters were insisting I visit a Dr Thomas, who had a surgery about seven miles away in a village we would be travelling through on our journey to Gumla. I told them nothing could be done for my back and that I'd suffered with it for years. The roads weren't helping, I said, and I probably wouldn't be better until I was off them altogether and back in England. But the sisters were adamant I should see Dr Thomas.

"He's such a nice man. I'm sure he can help you and he's such a caring person, too," said Sister Michael.

The ambulance pulled up outside this little brick building, the doctor's surgery. As it was after 11am the sisters wondered if he would still be there. Sister Vianney offered to go and find out.

"Stay there, Mr Brian. I will get him to come out and see you," she said. That was fine by me. Every move I made was causing me considerable pain, particularly getting in and out of the ambulance. Fortunately, or should I say unfortunately, the doctor was still there. As he came out to greet me it was obvious Sister Vianney had told him my name and with the broadest smile imaginable he said: "Good morning, Mr Brian. You are English, aren't you? How are you enjoying India?" By this time he had opened the passenger door and I managed a half-turn to shake his hand. "What's your problem?" he asked. I told him I'd had back trouble for years, often finding myself in great pain. I also said the dreadful roads had caused it to flare up by throwing me up and down. "Turn half round and pull your shirt up, please," he said, so I did, showing him my bare back with me facing the driver. I then told him where the pain usually was and, rather clumsily, I thought, he began feeling various areas of my back. I told him again where the pain was. During all this the sisters were watching his every move. I wouldn't have thought my back could have generated such interest. He continued to feel the wrong places and all at once I felt the worst pain it has ever been my misfortune to endure. This so-called doctor had evidently drawn his arm right back and, fist clenched, given my back, the most almighty wallop, which sent me sprawling into the driver's lap. I was seeing stars. The pain was excruciating. I was absolutely livid. You blithering fool, I remember saying quietly to myself. I could have used much stronger language, believe me, but there were nuns present so I bit my tongue. The amazing thing was that when he could see I was in so much pain he got quite excited.

"Mr Brian, Mr Brian," he repeated, "I know where your pain is. I've found it for you," he said, his voice rising in tone with the excitement. Having regained my composure, I turned to face him. He was smiling again. It was a smile that seemed to stretch from one side of his face to the other, showing the biggest white teeth imaginable.

"That hurt, didn't it? I can see you are in a lot of pain, but I'm pleased to say I've found it for you," he said. Still grimacing from the pain I was in, I looked at this doctor in disbelief. I'd told the fool where the pain was and he'd hit me there.

"Mr Brian, you have a very poor back. Your pain is caused by our dreadful roads and you won't be better until you get home to England," he said. This was getting ridiculous. I'd told him exactly what my problem was and he had told me nothing new. The only thing he had done was put me in even greater pain.

"Goodbye, Mr Brian. It was so nice to have met you, and do enjoy the remainder of your time in India, won't you," he said. I could have cried. It's a wonder he didn't break my back. If he's a caring doctor I hate to think what the others are like. As the ambulance pulled away from the village one of the sisters was heard to say: "He's such a nice man, isn't he?"

That journey to Gumla was a bit scary to say the least. A large lorry emblazoned with the words 'Good Luck' in capital letters very nearly hit our ambulance head-on. The driver of this lorry wouldn't give an inch and seemed to be heading straight for our vehicle. Only the quick reactions of our driver averted a major accident. The driving there has to be seen to be believed. Driving to Gumla that day we killed a dog and narrowly missed doing the same to three pigs and countless chickens. Some animals just don't move quickly enough. Big lorries would simply drive over the animal. Also on the road that day, I noted once again the exploitation of women. Occasionally one comes across road repairs and the ones we saw were being carried out by women, who were digging, shovelling, carrying, laying Tarmac and performing other extremely arduous tasks. There were about a dozen of them. The only man present was to be found sitting up in the steamroller, of which he was the driver. Those poor women. Some were teenage girls who would probably earn the equivalent of 15p for a day's hard graft. It must be back-breaking work for women. Some even had babies strapped to them, just to add to the strain. I couldn't believe what I was seeing amid the steam and the hot Tarmac. Wherever I've travelled in India I've always felt sorry for the women. The situation for them in the countryside is no different to that in the towns and cities. Women are third-class citizens here. Exploitation, so apparent to someone such as myself from England, is accepted as the norm in India. But in some states the exploitation of children is even worse. Even little children are employed to repair the roads. Children work long hours in carpet factories and brickworks for peanuts while their fat bosses get rich. The obnoxious caste system has a lot to answer for. Change is evidently on the way. One can only hope it is not centuries away.

At Gumla, once we had finally travelled the 18 miles in nearly three hours, it was time to say goodbye to Sister Angela. She had got out of the back of the ambulance and came round to the side passenger door, where the window was open. We shook hands and I even said we must definitely take that walk together some day. Have you ever seen a nun with sunglasses on? Well, that was Sister Angela, and she was looking quite glamorous. In the *My Indian Journey* book I had described Sister Angela as elegant. She had lost none of that quality. I really did appreciate her coming all that way to see me. Believe me, the pleasure had been all mine.

Before I was able to do some shopping we had to call at the Ursuline convent school in Gumla. The sisters in the ambulance had some work to attend to there. It was at this school, where there are now more than 1,800 pupils, that I once again met a charming white Belgian sister. I'd met her before when I last visited the school five years ago. She had been in India 47 years and her heart was obviously in that country. She had played a big part in the expansion of the school. I remember from last time how proud she was of her achievements. I'm not sure if she really recognised me, but I was made very welcome. On sitting down and talking to her she told me that in the whole of Bihar there was just her and one other white sister from Belgium left. All the others were Indian. I doubt very much if she will return to Belgium. She told me she would die in India. She was well into her 80s and her health had suffered since I last saw her. I'm sure she would have been unable to teach through poor health. She had found the strike extremely distressing and she was really happy that it was over, with the senior school children all now back in their classes. I particularly remembered this convent school because last time I was there I'd dashed to the toilet with diarrhoea, my trousers half down, with Sister Michael running after me. What a picture that still conjures up in the imagination. I remember collapsing on the toilet seat and laughing my head off, having just made it, with Sister Michael waiting patiently outside the toilet door. All she kept saying was "Are you alright, Mr Brian?" I also recall coming out of the toilet to be greeted by that same Belgian sister I was now chatting to once again. She had a pill in her hand. "Take this. You won't have trouble again. This pill will stop anything," she had said, smiling as she gave it to me. Sure enough, I never had the so-called Delhi Belly again.

Looking round the school, I got the usual courtesy from the Ursuline sisters. Some had remembered me. That school, like the others I had visited, was a happy place. The senior girls were obviously delighted to be back. What would India do without these convent schools? These marvellous sisters are giving thousands of children throughout Bihar an education. Only 40 per cent of all Indian children attend school, so 60 per cent are receiving no education whatsoever, which is really pitiful. Whenever I think of those Indian children who are among the unfortunate 60 per cent I automatically think of those thousands of street kids who roam Calcutta. If only they were to be given the chance that some of Bihar's children are getting. If only they could come under the love and protection that is so apparent in the Ursuline convent schools. I've said the words "if only" many times about India. If only those street kids, who had such a raw deal at birth, could at least have some hope. Instead of hope they have a degrading life, being spat at and kicked by the caste system. But in the country areas of Bihar there is hope and at the six convent schools I've visited in that state the hope shines through in the happiness of those children. Their hope may be only slight, but for the street kids there seems very little hope indeed.

After saying goodbye to the Ursuline sisters at Gumla it was time to go into the town for some shopping. I still had the four sisters from Tongo for company. I wouldn't have wanted to move too far without them, I can assure you, because this country town is literally overflowing with people. Thousands pack the streets, with the sacred cow for company. Chickens, pigs and all the other animals just seem to roam at will wherever they want. Among the muck, filth and smells there must be rats galore. It really is a scruffy, dirty place, with a population of probably 100,000 people. I've never seen so many miserable-looking dogs as there are in Gumla. They are literally skin and bones, their frames so pronounced on their skeletal bodies. Some are blind, some have three legs, some have the most terrible body sores it's ever been my misfortune to see and some appear to have no coats, their fur having seemingly disappeared. Death must be a blessing for them, indeed they can be seen dying all over this shabby country town. Indian people seem to have very little respect for these animals roaming their streets, except for the sacred cow, of course. It's as if they are just left to fend for themselves. In the shops the assistants were falling over themselves to serve me. I was white and had money - not much, mind you, but to them I might have been a millionaire. There are many bargains to be had in those shops and I would advise anyone never to pay the asking price. Haggle them down and you'll do a deal. I don't think I've ever been so conscious of the colour of my skin as I was in this town. I was looked at in a most peculiar way. In the restaurant, eyes never left me. I'm not sure if those people approved of me or not. The people in this outpost town just wouldn't see white people. It's hardly a tourist attraction, so there would be no reason for Westerners to visit. One must remember I was in deepest Bihar in a town straight out of the Wild West and well off the beaten track. Wherever I went people just stared at me. It was indeed a very strange feeling to be looked at the way I was that day.

After an uneventful journey back to Tongo and following the evening meal Sister Frederic entered my room.

"Mr Brian, I've come to see if I can help in any way with your back and I've brought Sister Harriet with me. She may be of use to you," she said. The time was 8.30pm and I was getting ready for bed, hoping too that I might at last get a good night's sleep. I hadn't slept at all well since arriving in Tongo. There had been far too many disturbances in the night and of course my back seemed if anything to have got worse. Sister Frederic was most concerned about it. Sister Harriet, all smiles and one of the newer sisters at Tongo, asked me to lie on my stomach on the bed. I might add that the only thing I was wearing was a pair of underpants. This sister would be about 38 and like some of the younger sisters at Tongo was quite good-looking. She proceeded to massage my back in a way I'd never experienced before. Who was this woman, I remember thinking. Her hands were digging into my back like no other had done before or since. Sister Frederic, who was watching the proceedings, told me Sister Harriet was a fully trained masseuse.

"You like, Mr Brian?" asked Sister Harriet. I told her I liked very much indeed. She was even better than Sister Sashila, and that's a real compliment. With the sides of her hands she was pounding away on my bare back She then asked me to turn over and began thumping the front of my body. After that she took my legs one at a time and lifted them as high as she could, lowering them and then pulling with all her might. Obviously I was getting the full works. She even got down to my toes and pulled at them, too.

"What on earth are you doing to me, Sister Harriet?" I remember asking. This was new to me - no one had ever pulled at my toes before. All Sister Frederic kept saying was "Isn't she good." I then asked this sister if she'd have a look at my bad ankle, which was the reason I'd stopped playing cricket. She then concentrated all her resources on it and here again she treated it like no one ever had. This trained masseuse who happened to be an Ursuline nun really was one of the divine sisters. In my excitement I could even see myself making a comeback at cricket. I would be able to run again. But all good things eventually come to an end and Sister Frederic said that was enough. She also said she would bring Sister Harriet to see me again the following evening. As they both said good night I felt at peace with the world. My body felt as though it were on fire, yet I felt perfectly relaxed. A lovely glowing feeling was sweeping my body. This was to be a perfect, painless night's sleep. I was just drifting off when the most hideous animal noises started up again. This time there seemed to be hundreds out there. So much for a good night's sleep.

It was, without doubt, the worst night I experienced at Tongo. What sort of animals were they? The sisters had told me there were only a few dogs at the school and certainly not the 50 I thought there were at first. So what were those noises? They were certainly animals. Sometimes I felt they were just below my bedroom window. As I write this book in the comfort of my own home I can only assume that those animal noises were coming from the forests, which were very close to the school. There must have been scores of animals there and at night they would come looking for food. To lie in your bed in the Indian sub-continent and hear all sorts of animals can be a scary experience, particularly at the dead of night when everything is pitch dark. Those strange howling noises went on all night and a squadron of mosquitoes also decided to pay me a visit. There must have been hundreds of them buzzing round my mosquito net. That buzz can also seem very loud in the middle of the night. Some actually got under the net and goodness only knows how many times I was bitten. I couldn't get from under the net because once I was out in the open they would really descend on me. So I just lay there and thought of rats. I thought of the hundreds of rats that would be out scurrying all over the school, on the roofs just above my bedroom and outside the window. Then, at about 4am, the barking, or whatever it was, stopped. The mosquitoes flew off elsewhere and everywhere was quiet again. But then at 4.40am the big bell clangs away to wake up the school and within minutes the place is alive with the chatter of children, while the sisters can be heard singing in the chapel. I hadn't slept a wink that night and I was really beginning to feel dreadfully tired.

On my last whole day at Tongo I sat with the sisters at breakfast feeling absolutely shattered. With not sleeping properly and not eating too well either I was beginning to lose weight. Not that I didn't particularly like the food that was put before me. It was just as though I wasn't hungry. Sister Alphonsa, the cook for the sisters, did her best to get me eating. She even gave me specially prepared English meals, bless her. But, for reasons I can't be sure of, I just lost my appetite.

Some of the sisters were giggling about the noises they had heard coming from my room the previous evening when Sister Harriet had been with me. Sister Vianney, who was sitting next to me and had washed and dressed me that morning, found it all highly amusing. I knew I would get my leg pulled unmercifully again. The sisters' wicked sense of humour was in full swing. Here I was, propped up with the usual water bottle at my back, probably feeling a bit sorry for myself, while the conversation went something like this.

Sister Michael, a smile on her face, said: "Mr Brian, the reason why you are in such pain is because God loves you."

I looked at her and replied: "Why me, then, what have I done wrong?"

"The more pain you are in, the more he loves you," she said.

"Thank you very much," I retorted.

"Perhaps God is punishing you with this pain you are having in your back because of what you said about the chief government minister of Bihar," said a sister further down the breakfast table. By now, all of them were laughing.

"But I didn't mean it when I said I wanted to break his other leg," I protested.

"Well, you said it, though, didn't you?" said Sister Michael. Everyone was by now in stitches.

"You shouldn't have had such evil thoughts," added another voice from down the table.

"Well, some of you weren't thinking too highly of the chief minister either, were you?" I replied.

"That's true," they said as one.

"You weren't too sympathetic when you heard he had

broken his leg. Perhaps your pain is to come," I continued.

"Did you know that the chief minister's 14-year-old daughter fell down and broke her leg as well?" asked Sister Scholastica.

"You're joking," I said, genuinely surprised.

"It's true. She slipped and broke her leg," related Sister Alphonsa.

"Answer me this, then. That girl had done nothing wrong. Why should she have been punished like that?" I asked.

"God moves in mysterious ways," was Sister Vianney's reply.

"I understand the poor girl broke her leg at home on a slippery floor," added another sister.

"Well, well," I said, getting really excited, "it's the chief minister who should have broken his other leg on the slippery floor. That accident wasn't meant for his daughter, but for him. God meant to punish him, not his daughter. There's been a mistake," I said.

"What? God's mistake?" I was asked.

"Maybe", I said, as the conversation continued in its lighthearted vein.

"Mr Brian, no wonder you are in great pain. You really shouldn't say things like that because you may well now be in even greater pain. He will be most displeased with you, but whatever pain you are in and however great it is, always remember that God loves you," said Sister Michael, smiling broadly.

Everyone else was laughing their heads off. I was laughing so much that I'd forgotten about my back. When I talked about God's "mistake", the sisters could hardly take in what I was saying. They looked at me in disbelief. All at once I doubled up in pain, caused simply by laughing too much. I was in agony once more.

"Always remember - the greater the pain, the more He

loves you," said Sister Michael again. It really was highly amusing. God was punishing me, according to the sisters, and they were laughing about it.

Sister Margaret Mary, the principal of the school and the one in overall charge, had returned to Tongo. She had been on a religious retreat for a few days. I feel as though I've known her for years. She seemed to have settled perfectly into the position of principal. What an interesting lady she is. I could talk to her all day. Unfortunately, with her being away from Tongo, I hadn't seen a lot of her. But what I had seen I liked very much indeed. She took over at Tongo from Sister Albina Dungoung, who was principal when I last came. I kept in touch with Sister Albina by letter. She is at a convent school in north east India, not too far from the Chinese border. It's so remote there that wild elephants come out of the forest and do untold damage to their vegetables. Not only are the elephants hungry, but they tread all over the vegetable garden and it's a constant worry for the sisters. Without these precious vegetables they're finished - it's starvation, just as it would be at the other convent schools I've visited. Sister Albina also told me that all Westerners are banned from that part of the world because it is so remote and dangerous. Had I decided to visit her it would have been a journey of over 300 miles. Although we tend to think of India as an overcrowded country, we forget there are also extremely remote areas where very few white people have visited. It is in one such area that Sister Albina is now living.

That last day in Tongo was spent walking around the school grounds and visiting classrooms, and I have to inform you, reader, that Ba-Ba Black Sheep and Jack and Jill are very much in evidence in these convent schools in deepest Bihar. The British Empire not only left Victorian-style buildings in the towns and cities, laid roads and railways and brought law and order, but it also brought nursery rhymes to countless schools. Wherever I've been in India, whether on the first trip or the second, I've been most conscious of the spirit of the British Raj. In the big cities you just can't escape it. It's all around you. Out in the countryside it is, admittedly, not so noticeable. But to hear nursery rhymes being sung by Indian children really does bring home to a visitor such as myself what Britain was to India and indeed, I might add, what it still is. I've never heard any criticism of the British. In fact it's just the opposite. Indians are grateful for what Britain did for them. I'm not saying for one moment that they all think that way, but I can only speak as I find and in an unusual way it has made me feel quite proud to be British. I found it very strange to be hearing those nursery rhymes sung in English, as the children can't speak English, but a little bit of the Old Country is still very much present in today's Indian countryside. And judging by the faces of the children singing those nursery rhymes, there can be no happier children anywhere.

When I think of Indian schools, not just Tongo but the others I've visited, I cannot fail to make a comparison with the schools in Britain today. Not being a schoolteacher, of course, one has to rely on newspapers to discover what's going on in our schools. Why is it, I ask myself and anyone reading this book, that children from the poorest homes imaginable are so perfectly well behaved. Those children in the Indian countryside love going to school. Not all of them get the chance, of course, and many still have to stay at home to help their parents in the fields. The ones who do go to school are the lucky ones and they seem to appreciate what they've been given. At any time during my stay in Tongo I could have walked into a classroom and sensed such intense effort being put in to learning that you could have heard a pin drop, such would have been the silence and concentration. There is no violence at Tongo school and no truancy either, just happy, studious children who are so keen to learn. Sometimes there might be 50 of them to a classroom. In England we are told that if a class has 30 pupils in it a teacher can't manage. I'm sure there could be 100 pupils in an Indian classroom and you would still find the most well-behaved children imaginable. I know that in England if it's news we hear it tends to be bad news. Good news, like children behaving correctly in classrooms, doesn't make the headlines. When one reads of a London headmaster being knifed to death outside his school gates, of teachers in Halifax refusing to teach 60 children who are out of control and of some schools in England where teachers fear for their lives, it gives cause for alarm. Juvenile delinquency is very much in evidence in English schools. Discipline starts in the home. The discipline for Indian children in those little huts is very strict. They respect their parents. In some cases couples do separate, but the vast majority of children are in close-knit, loving families. Married couples do generally stay together, which must benefit the children. Look at single mothers in England today. Some may have children by three different men, who opt out of all responsibility for the children, leaving the poor mother to bring them up on her own. Is that the proper way to raise children? I do believe that in England today some children do not know the difference between right and wrong. If fathers are not at home to instil discipline, this to me is where the problem lies. I know there are a lot of single mothers who bring up their children quite successfully, but a child instinctively needs both a father and mother. In India I've seen some of the most beautifully-behaved children it's ever been my pleasure to behold. I'd love to see some school teacher friends of mine walk into those Indian classrooms. "The pleasure's all mine," they would say to me. From what we read in our English newspapers, teachers can't leave the profession fast enough.

They have had enough. If there's no discipline at home, some children can be young thugs when they start school and it's left to the teacher to try to control them, which in some cases is impossible. Out in the Indian countryside it's so different. Have we progressed so much in England that we can't control our children any more? If that's progress, we are the poorer for it.

Being at Tongo for the second time, I've got to know the school teachers quite well. I knew before that there were some who worked part-time and I assumed that the Ursuline sisters, all being teachers, were the only qualified ones, but I was wrong. I discovered that there are nearly 20 full-time teachers. I had not really come into contact with them before, but I did on my second visit. These teachers would all live in Tongo, or another nearby village, in their little mud huts, just like the peasant farmers. All of them are college-trained, some are married with children and all are women. But even though they are clever enough to go to college, it does not alter the fact that they are from the lower castes. Although they may feel, like Albina Kujur, that they are one step up the social ladder, they are still lower-caste and there is no getting away from it. Having made such progress, one would have thought these teachers earned a decent wage, but they are shockingly paid. Having said that, they would of course be earning more money than anyone else in their village. For them, though, just like the rest of the lower castes, there is no escape. India won't allow it.

These teachers went out of their way to welcome me into their school. With the senior girls now back in classes, I was invited to the school hall to meet them. There were 600 pupils in that hall, all of them obviously delighted to be back after the strike. Singing and dancing was being presented for my enjoyment. It was The Sound of Music all over again. I'm sure the singing of those senior girls would have been heard miles away. The hills in the Tongo area would be alive with music again. After the entertainment, the principal asked for questions from the audience, with her acting as interpreter as the girls spoke Hindi. Many questions were asked in particular about the British royal family. Indians really are interested in our royals. I hope I gave satisfactory answers. One question, though, was telling about today's India, not to mention being unwittingly close to the bone about politics in Britain. A girl of about 16 asked: "Are British politicians as corrupt as Indian politicians?" I thought long and hard about this particular question and remember saying that I was sure there was some corruption in British politics but that it wasn't on the same massive scale as that seen in India. If I had been perfectly honest I could have mentioned that the sleaze issue was getting out of control in the Conservative Party. Many MPs had admitted to having affairs and the Cash for Questions scandal had rocked Parliament. One MP had actually admitted receiving payment for asking a question in the Commons. Far be it for me to criticise Tory MPs for such human failings. We all have such temptations, don't we, and we can all be lured off the straight and narrow. As I write, the Conservative Party has faced up to a humiliating defeat in the General Election and I'm certain sleaze played a part in bringing down the government. But who was I to criticise my own country while abroad? Whatever party is in power, be it Labour or Conservative, one should never criticise them while in another country. Let foreigners criticise us if they wish. That is their prerogative. It was not unlike the situation I found myself in while on National Service in Hong Kong. When abroad, either as soldier or civilian, one should defend one's country to the greatest possible degree. There may well have been corruption in the Conservative Party, but I wasn't prepared to admit to more than that.

For a young Indian schoolgirl to have asked such a question was quite extraordinary, because being in the outback of India those children wouldn't have access to newspapers to read of such things as corruption. They certainly wouldn't have TV at home and it's highly doubtful that there would be radio either. So how would those senior schoolgirls know of the corruption that is is widespread throughout India? This corruption in Indian politics must be far-reaching, because even the tribal people know it's going on. Many questions were asked in that hall that day. The enthusiasm of the children told me how interested they were in anything to do with Britain. They really have put the Old Country on a pedestal, and their own country's long association with Britain will never be forgotten in those Indian schools. There persists a strange and quite fascinating relationship with Britain which, hopefully, will never die. Obviously, the British Raj lies at the root of it. These children wanted to know as much about my country as possible. They seemed so intelligent and my real hope for them when they leave school is that they can go on to make something of themselves, just like Albina Kujur has done. In many respects they are the lucky children of this part of Bihar. Others would be going without an education altogether, born to work in the rice fields and remain illiterate forever.

Sister Sabina is the youngest Ursuline nun at Tongo. I'd say she was about 28. Being a nun is perfect for her. I have said before that I regard the Ursuline sisters as near-perfect human beings and in fact their life demands that they are so, but Sister Sabina - and I mustn't make her blush - is also extremely attractive. A more loving and caring sister it would be hard to find, and I say that having met the most loving, caring people it's ever been my pleasure to know. I'd asked her if she cared to walk with me to the river bridge about a quarter of a mile from the main school gates. I always felt that if I wanted to get any of the sisters to talk to me about themselves and their lives it was best tried one to one. Also, of course, it was good research for this book. I wanted to know why this person had wanted to become a nun. In many ways it was like talking to Sister Angela again. She was probably not quite as frank, but this kind and gentle sister gave me total honesty. If God had called her to serve Him, He couldn't have chosen better. Like Sister Angela she had this great desire to become an Ursuline nun and serve the Catholic church. She traced this back to a very early age. Sister Sabina admitted that while growing up she was attracted to boys, but this in itself did not give her satisfaction. She told me she was born into a quite well-off middle-caste family. She had everything, but something was lacking. She knew what she wanted and nothing was going to stop her. She is now completely happy and contented with her chosen vocation. Like all these Brides of Christ, she is dedicated to God and the idea of serving him for the rest of her life. Like all the other sisters, her life is complete. I'm sure Sister Sabina, Sister Angela and countless other Ursuline sisters would have made wonderful wives because their natures are so loving. But they have forsaken the traditional way of life for their desire to serve God. The dictionary definition of the word divine includes the words 'of supreme excellence or worth' and I can't improve on that in describing the Ursuline sisters. Sister Sabina, who I believe is yet to take her final vows, is to me perfectly cut out for being an Ursuline sister.

Have you ever experienced something in life that was so wonderful it will stay with you forever? Do you have those moments that will never leave you, moments that as you get older will always be there, implanted in the memory forever? I'm sure we have all experienced precious moments. I can list a few, like getting married and the birth of my two children (for any man, the arrival of children is something he'll never forget) and to a lesser extent the birth of my three grandchildren. Meeting Albina Kujur for the first time at Ranchi Airport was another such moment. On the sporting side, getting that first hundred at cricket will live with me forever, not that I scored that many, and I was ecstatic when that first London Marathon medal was hung round my neck, particularly as I'd done it for Tongo. Believe me when I say I know what it must be like to score the winning goal at Wembley. But what happened to me that last late afternoon at Tongo was equally as good as any of the things I've just mentioned. This was indeed a very special moment. Sometimes I do get quite emotional and perhaps as I get older I am becoming more sentimental, but this moment brought tears to my eyes and when I think about it even now it still does.

As Sister Sabina and I walked back to the school gates along the very dusty road that runs alongside the grounds, we passed a little lane which is nearly opposite the school. I remembered it well because at the bottom of it was where Shashi, that little undernourished girl, lived. She, of course, was the frightened youngster who lived next door to her tyrannical uncle. Just as we walked by this lane, who should come walking up it but Shashi. Evidently, she had been back to her home, gathered up all her possessions and placed them in a blanket, tying it up into a bundle with string. In this blanket she was carrying her life. This poor seven-year-old with the staring eyes was a pitiful sight. The blanket she was carrying looked bigger than her. But I could at last see the glimmer of a smile as she saw me. That day she had been to school for the first time in many weeks. She had gone home to collect what she had and was returning to school. Sister Sabina quickly got talking to her. I couldn't, of course, because she wouldn't have understood me. Sister Sabina told me that Shashi's sister Nina had returned home from Ranchi that day. By some miracle she had found her mother among the teeming masses there, but had promptly been sent home. Her mother didn't want her any more. The only friend she would have in the world would be Shashi, her sister. I asked Sister Sabina to ask Shashi if she would fetch Nina. This she did, setting off on the 400 yards back to where they both lived. After Sister Sabina and I had stood about at the top of this lane for about five minutes, two of the smallest girls possible appeared in the evening light way off in the distance, virtually at the bottom of the lane. It must be said that until this point I hadn't even met Nina. The two of them were not walking very quickly and I wondered whether Nina would be too shy to come to me. All at once I shouted in English "Come on, then." Hearing this, the sisters started to run to me. I don't know how they understood what I'd shouted at them, but it was quickly clear that it was a race between them to see who would get to me first. They were neck and neck as they got closer to me. Both girls were laughing as they raced towards me. I was kneeling down by then and Nina made it first into my arms, with Shashi a close second. Shashi must have told her sister that they would both be boarding at the Tongo school. When those two excitable children ran into my arms it really was a moment to savour. Without question, it was one of the greatest feelings of my life. I felt I had the whole world in my arms. "They are mine," I said to myself as I carried them into the school. They really were as light as a feather and terribly undernourished. Allow me, if you will, to indulge in a little self-satisfaction. I'd beaten the bully. I'd won. And it felt so good, so very, very good - so triumphantly good. Those two children would be abused no more. The dreaded uncle was a thing of the past. At last both those kids were laughing. Believe me when I say it was worth covering all the thousands of miles I'd travelled to get to India to see those two unhappy children smiling again. I also knew that as boarders at the school they would not only be getting an education but also the love and concern for their welfare that the sisters would be giving them.

That evening I sat down at the dining table with the sisters for my last evening meal with them. I'd attended the school chapel just beforehand with the sisters for a short service taken by the priest of Tongo village. Prayers were said for my safe return home. It was, in many respects, a sad evening for me personally because the next day I would be leaving them. But laughter was never far away. I happened to tell Sister Michael that my back was much better.

"I told you God loves you, didn't I," she said with a smile. I went on to say that since Sister Harriet had started massaging my back there had been big improvement.

"She's the best ever," I remember saying as I smiled at Sister Harriet. Sister Vianney, sitting at my side, nearly choked on her soup at that remark. I can speak from experience, as three nuns have massaged my back - Sister Harriet, Sister Sushila and Sister Vianney. Surely this must be some kind of record - to have had a body massage from three different Ursuline nuns. I have indeed been most fortunate, I can tell you. I know I can say this in the nicest possible way. Knowing them the way I do, I know no offence will be taken. They would simply roar with laughter, and they also know I would do or say nothing to harm them in any way. On the contrary, I would in fact move mountains to help them. That's how much I think of them.

"It's not what I have done for you, but what you've done for me that counts," I told Sister Margaret Mary and the other sisters on that last evening, when I also told them I wanted to continue helping the school by improving the facilities in some areas, which are deteriorating rapidly. We were talking over our last supper, so to speak, on my very last evening with the Divine Sisters. I know my life is much richer for having met them. Before I went to India the first time I doubt if I had ever spoken to a nun in my life. Having passed them in the street they always seemed somehow distant. I imagined most of their lives would be taken up in prayer, which of course turned out to be true. They never seemed to smile much, either, and, being nuns, they would, I thought, be completely embroiled in their commitment to God. So imagine what a delightful surprise it was to discover that nuns have as good a sense of humour as anyone I've met. The wicked sense of humour of the nuns in Tongo borders on the hilarious. Meeting them has certainly altered my life because I realise that material things are just not important in this world. What is important, and what these sisters undoubtedly have, is love for other human beings. They have an abundance of love, a Christian love. If everyone in this world had this love that the Ursuline sisters possess, I can positively state that there would be no more wars. Surely that is something we could all strive for.

The speeches over, I had a surprise for the sisters. While shopping with Sister Vianney in Gumla I had asked her what I should buy for the sisters. On her advice, it was decided to buy each one a head scarf. With shrieks of delight each sister put on their scarf. I knew I'd done the right thing. I did so want to buy them something. As they do not even see the money they earn they would not even have the luxury of buying a simple head scarf. The 16 sisters then began singing, their beautiful voices flowing not only through that dining room but through the whole school and out into the darkness of Bihar. They were singing to me and I had a lump in my throat. How could I ever forget such people who had been so good to me? How could I ever repay them? At 8.30pm I retired to my bedroom for my last night in Tongo. The lump in my throat wasn't moving easily and I felt choked. Staying at that school again had been such a wonderful experience. Seeing such well-behaved children is something I will never forget. That Tongo school is a special place, believe me, and I know I shall think of it for the rest of my life. What a lovely welcome everyone had given me. My love for those Divine Sisters of Tongo is very strong indeed and that last night at the school was touched with sadness. I was leaving them the following day. I went up the stairs so slowly, followed by Sister Frederic and Sister Harriet. I'd said good night to the other sisters, but these two had promised me another massage. "One final massage, Mr Brian," Sister Frederic had said.

Lying on my bed, I really was given a full-scale body massage. This was the final once-over, my last massage at Tongo, with lots of thumping, pushing, stretching and grunting. If Sister Harriet wanted to leave an everlasting impression on me then she was succeeding. I was absolutely convinced that I had the finest masseuse in all India at my disposal. While I was lying on my stomach with Sister Harriet pushing and probing my bare back, Sister Frederic, who has such a quiet voice, whispered in my ear, saying Sister Harriet knew a lot about people's bodies. Well, she certainly knew a lot about mine. She knew all my strengths and weaknesses and after that remark by Sister Frederic I couldn't stop laughing, particularly when Sister Harriet, who was by then pulling one of my legs, said "You like, Mr Brian?" She really was proving to be my Jewel in the Crown. What a photo that would have made. How hilariously funny it must have looked. Here I was, half-naked on my bed, being attended to in the arts of body massage by, of all people, two Ursuline nuns, one of them giving me a sort of pleasurable torture and the other whispering sweet words in my ear. The other sisters could be heard giggling in their rooms about what was going on. How could I ever forget such moments. I've had many highs and lows during my experiences in India, but what was happening on that bed was undoubtedly one of the highs. I laughed and laughed and even now, many months later, I'm still laughing about that particular incident. The good news was that my back was on the mend. The magic of the finest masseuse in India had straightened me out, so to speak. The pain was gradually receding and hopefully I'd be alright for the long road journey back to Ranchi the next day. Out in the subcontinent of India, in deepest Bihar in the village of Tongo I was fast realising that I'd found a real diamond in Sister Harriet.

Chapter Nine

Miracles

Goodbyes can be sad occasions, and the day I left Tongo certainly fell into that category. As the ambulance sped down that slight hill on which the village stands I was choked. My farewell reminded me so much of my previous visit. When I'd left the school that time, the scene had been exactly the same. All the Ursuline sisters, all the teachers and probably a quarter of the school children had seen me off. As I passed through those brand new gates I wondered anew whether I would ever visit again. Who knows what the future holds? With me in the ambulance were Sister Margaret Mary, Sister Scholastica, Sister Michael and Sister Vianney. These four would be seeing me off next day from Ranchi Airport. Looking back on that last night in Tongo, I desperately wanted a good night's sleep. With all that travelling ahead of me I really needed it. The mosquitoes had other ideas, though. Once again, some got inside my net. Just as well I was taking malaria tablets. I must have been bitten many hundreds of times during my time at Tongo. At the breakfast table I felt really drained and tired. I'd only spent just over a week at the school and it was certainly having some effect on my health. I just longed for sleep, but I'd been unable to get it.

Sister Frederic had insisted that, because of the amount of time I was to spend in the ambulance, I must have a hot water bottle on my back. I was fortunate always to have been placed in the front passenger seat, which was far more comfortable than where the sisters sat inside the ambulance. As I was getting that frantic farewell, I couldn't help but think of all the memories of Tongo, not only the school but the whole area. And here I was seeing the spectacular colours of the Bihar countryside for the last time. The sheer beauty of that part of Bihar had added to the mystique of Tongo. I'd found such peace there that I couldn't begin to explain its precise meaning. I knew it was an idyllic spot to be at. Apart from the mosquitoes and those strange howling noises at night, that is.

One feature of India I won't miss is its dreadful roads. Once again I was in some discomfort, but I knew from experience that my back was getting better and, once in the ambulance, we made very good time on the route to Gumla. The town was, as I'd come to expect, overflowing with people. I have many memories of Gumla, but cleanliness is not one of them. It really is the dirtiest of all Indian towns I have seen. The disease found there must be immense. It's probably existed that way for the last 100 years. It seems to be a place that time forgot, but there are probably hundreds of other towns like it all over India, located, like Gumla, in the far-flung heart of the countryside. Apart from the shops there is a bank, but I certainly saw no evidence of any industry. Gumla could well be one of those towns to where the peasant farmers from the Tongo area regularly come to sell their home-grown vegetables on the streets for a miserly sum of money which, naturally, they are most grateful for.

The ambulance proceeded towards Lohardaga. We didn't have to go there, because it wasn't on the main route to Ranchi, but I'd requested we go that way because I wanted once again to meet Sister Angeline. This sister is not to be confused with Sister Angela, of Samtoli convent school. Sister Angeline was the principal of the Ursuline training college when I last visited Lohardaga. The bright, or should I say lucky, children of the area, Albina Kujur among them, would attend this college. Those who come here would indeed be among the most fortunate of all children from the countryside. Having done well at school, they would hopefully get to college. If a peasant farmer's daughter attended college it really would mean she was trying to make something of herself. Albina, through her own efforts, had made it to the Lohardaga college, moving there from the Ursuline convent school at Tongo. Here again, as with a lot of the schools in Bihar, the college is run by Ursuline sisters. When I'd visited it before, I'd realised how lucky Albina had been in having Sister Angeline as principal to keep an eye on her. This sister had always given her every possible encouragement. I think she was just as determined as Albina that she should become a school teacher. Right from the early days of my sponsoring her, it had been Albina's ambition to attend college. Sister Angeline could see how much it meant to me that she should do well there. When I'd first met Albina, I mentioned how frail I thought she looked. I could see she certainly wasn't a robust type. "Do not worry, Mr. Brian. I will keep a special eye on her for you," Sister Angeline had said. Albina had been so desperate to achieve her ambition to become a school teacher when I last saw her, so, more than anything else, I wanted to see this sister again and thank her personally for what she'd done for Albina.

When, after four years at the college, Albina had finally passed her exams to become a teacher, Sister Angeline had even arranged an interview for her at Bihar Sharif. She was over the moon when she was told there and then that she had got the job. She was a school teacher at last. My purpose in seeing Sister Angeline, though, was not just to thank her for all she'd done in helping Albina, but to find out how she had beaten cancer. The sisters at Tongo had told me her extraordinary story. She was gravely ill with terminal cancer and had been given just a few weeks to live at the most. But through prayer and her obvious belief in God she had made a complete and remarkable recovery. She had defied the tremendous odds stacked against her. How could she have made a complete nonsense of being at death's door, going from literally waiting and expecting to die to making such a marvellous recovery? How had she done it? Could great powers of prayer have released her from near death and given her back her life as a normal, healthy human being? She was no youngster. She wasn't even middle-aged. She would have been in her 70s, and death would probably not be unexpected for an Indian person of her age. Maybe less than three per cent of India's vast population would be expected to make the age of 70, so if anyone in this world was ready for death, it would probably be Sister Angeline. She might, in all probability, have been looking forward to dying and as a nun she would be better prepared than most. Her time in this world would be up and she would be starting to think beyond it and of life in the next. These are the very words she used when speaking to me. Death holds no fears for Ursuline sisters, believe me.

It was at the Lohardaga Training College that I met Sister Angeline again. Because of her age she had retired three years previously as principal, but she still lived there. She didn't even know I was in India and I took her completely by surprise. We found her in the dining room having a cup of tea. As I went up to her, she gave me the most old-fashioned look possible. It told me what she was thinking: "It's not you?" she seemed to be saying. After recognising me, though, she immediately thanked me for her copy of *My Indian Journey*, which she'd received during our correspondence over the last five years. I felt it was the least I could do, simply because she had been so good to Albina.

"Your book - I did so enjoy it. It was like a tonic to me while I was ill, and didn't it make me laugh," she said. I complimented her on how well she looked. She looked remarkable. Nobody would ever have thought that just a few months earlier she had been dying. I then thanked her most sincerely for the way she had taken such a close interest in Albina. She admitted she was very fond of her.

"She's a lovely girl. Do you know, when I was ill she came all the way from Bihar Sharif to visit me. She is such a caring person. You must be extremely proud of her," said Sister Angeline. I replied that I most definitely was proud of her. "Look how well she did in her exams. She worked so very hard to pass and I was so thrilled for her when she was appointed a school teacher in Bihar Sharif. Nobody deserves it more than she does," continued Sister Angeline, who for me is undoubtedly one of the Divine Sisters. It really was Albina's good fortune to have had her as principal at the college during her four years there. I know some of the country folk in the wilds of India do not get much luck in their lives. To be born into such poverty is hardship enough. But to have met Sister Angeline had indeed been Albina's slice of luck. That dear lady had gone way beyond her duties as principal to look after one of her students and I tried to show my gratitude by visiting her at the college. I know she appreciated my calling on her - and she was one among many I'd wished to see again on my second trip to India.

As we sat in that dining room she told me how she had overcome cancer.

"For many months I hadn't been well. I was deteriorating rapidly and it was then that I was told I had stomach cancer," she said, adding: "My only hope was an operation to remove the cancer, which I eventually had in Bombay, but it wasn't successful and I returned to Lohardaga to die. I was given just a few weeks to live."

But, being an Ursuline nun, she naturally had an overwhelming faith in God. "I certainly wasn't afraid to die, but prayer helped me enormously," she said. On coming back from Bombay she was absolutely certain she was going to die, though of course prayer, which the Ursuline sisters spend many hours a day engaged in, would have brought her great comfort. She then heard of religious retreats, which were being held all over India. They had proved to be highly successful and word about them spread like wildfire, literally sweeping the country. Miracles were apparently being performed.

The Tongo sisters had told me about these retreats before and they believed in them most emphatically. People were coming from all over the world to attend and spectacular results were being produced. Thousands of people had been to the retreats and hundreds had been cured, making remarkable recoveries. This had happened to the sick and the injured. Even cripples had started walking again. For people like Sister Angeline, literally at death's door, these recoveries had been nothing short of miraculous.

She had decided to attend one at Lohardaga out of curiosity, and once there she found many people in a much worse state than her. Many thousands of people who, like Sister Angeline, were terminally ill, gathered in an open field.

"Many priests were preaching the word of God and speaking about healing. Lots of people there had all kinds of dreadful diseases and were sure to die. But the people in that field were being told that providing they came over to God completely and were prepared to start a new life, renouncing their sins, they could be cured. But it was no use hoping for a miracle if you didn't believe. God wouldn't help you. He would only help those who were sincere, which meant total commitment to Him. They were being told 'give yourself to Him and start a new life'," recalled Sister Angeline. So in that large field that day she knelt and prayed, not necessarily for herself but for the crowds of desperately ill people who were there. The results of attending the retreat were astonishing. Within days she began feeling better. "It was an absolutely miraculous recovery - a miracle, nothing less than a miracle," she said. Again she emphasised that she thought she was about to die. "Yet, today I'm a new woman. There's no other explanation. It was the work of God," she said quite excitedly. "I feel wonderful," she said, and believe me, she looked it.

At Tongo the sisters had given me a popular mission magazine called Vechanolsavam. Featured in it were real-life instances of people who, having attended the retreats, had made miraculous recoveries. They had been born again, said the sisters. "We have heard of such success at these retreats that they must be God's work," they said. Sister Angeline needs no convincing by anyone that miracles are being performed. Indeed, she is herself a walking miracle who has confounded doctors who might not believe in such phenomena. Reading this mission magazine after returning home, there really would seem to be examples of incredible recoveries by people in a hopeless condition, with no apparent possibility of improvement. Without trying to convert anyone to Christianity, I feel there definitely is such success in these religious retreats. They simply demand attention. Allow me to quote just one example from this magazine. A man had been in a terrible accident when a heavy lump of concrete fell on his back. He was in permanent, excruciating pain, which doctors couldn't control. As time went by it spread down his right leg. He was admitted to hospital again and became very weak. The pain was so intense that it deprived him of sleep. He was told it would be with him for life. Because of his condition he contemplated suicide. He had lost the will to live and wanted to be out of all pain. He then heard about the religious retreats and, out of curiosity, attended one. He prayed that Christ would heal him. At the end of the Holy Mass, the priest announced the healing of back pains for eight people, and the man then felt something very heavy being removed from his back.

From that moment the pain left him. God had healed him completely. Obviously he was just one among many who had a great faith in God. The magazine is full of similar stories. It really was quite unbelievable that not so long ago Sister Angeline was dying. But she emphasised to me several times that it was no use hoping for a miracle if you didn't believe in God.

"Miracles will only be performed if you are a believer," she had said. And how do I feel about what I've read and been told about these religious retreats? I've actually met someone who has made such a marvellous recovery. The sisters at Tongo were absolutely convinced it was the work of God. It must be so, because so many people had been cured, they kept telling me. Sister Angeline was right when she said a miracle had been performed on her. And because of her complete recovery and the success of those retreats, I believe in miracles, too.

It was Sister Angeline who had first told me about the violence in Bihar, particularly in the area round Lohardaga. She had told me when I first met her five years ago that a gang of thugs had raided her college convent school. A gun had been pressed to her throat. "One wrong move and I'd have been dead," she had told me. Evidently, these gangs not only loot the places they attack, but also inspire great fear wherever they go. Sister Angeline also told me that even though the college had a big eight-foot wall all around it and security guards, nothing was completely secure. I came away from the college the first time thinking what a vulnerable position the sisters there were in, particularly in the case of the young girl students, of which of course Albina was then one. After I'd sent Sister Angeline my book she wrote back to say that if she had known I was writing a book she could have told me of a lot more cases where law and order had completely broken down. "Yes, Lohardaga today is a dangerous place," she had said. While there this second time I shuddered at the thought that even with such a high wall and security guards those attending and living at the college were not assured of safety. It made me think of the wall that circles the convent school at Tongo, which as a result is safer than it's ever been. But it is certainly not a fortress and people, whoever they may be, could quite easily break into the school. Violence is increasing in many parts of Bihar, and Lohardaga wouldn't have experienced the violence which seems to be out of control in North Bihar. Against this background of increasing trouble I can only hope and pray that Tongo remains peaceful. It seems that way at present and I sincerely hope it stays that way.

Lohardaga looked very much like a typical Indian town. It reminded me a lot of Gumla, looking equally dirty. The population is 50,000 and hordes of people throng the streets. The peasant farmer was again to be seen selling vegetables he'd grown on his plot of village land. I'd loved to have spoken to Sister Angeline considerably longer. She is such an interesting conversationalist and I'm sure she would have told me a lot more about life in Lohardaga, her English being near-perfect. As we said our farewells and shook hands she said: "Now don't forget, Mr Brian, if you write another book, please send me one so I can have another good laugh."

So, off the ambulance rattled again through the streets of Lohardaga and out into the countryside once more. We had only been in that college about an hour, but by speaking to Sister Angeline again I felt I'd learnt such a lot in such a short space of time. Her words "it's a miracle" were still ringing in my ears. Sister Vianney had wanted the ambulance to get to Ranchi in good time. "We have much to do there," she said. I'm not surprised the ambulance seems to be forever breaking down. With those deplorable roads, I'm sure that the jolting of the wheels over those potholes will eventually cause all the nuts and bolts holding the vehicle together to work loose. But, bad roads or not, my back was much better. The finest masseuse in all India had worked wonders on me. I was, at last, comfortable in that passenger seat and I certainly had a lot to thank Sister Harriet for.

After negotiating those awful roads, the ambulance finally made it to Ranchi. At the Ursuline convent school there I was met once again by Sister Bernadette, who would be one of the group of Ursuline sisters seeing me off the next day at the airport. Ranchi is the headquarters, so to speak, of the Order of St. Ursula in South Bihar. This is the convent where all the sisters would congregate for mass services, seminars, meetings and interviews. It also had by far the largest number of pupils in that part of the state. All the school children in South Bihar would have to go there for important exams. Walking round that school and seeing hundreds of school children and also the many sisters who live there, it looks quite impressive. The school buildings are imposing and the chapel is quite beautiful. I thought again of those four Belgian sisters who arrived in Ranchi in 1901 to educate Indian school children. The Order of St. Ursula has come a long way since those early dark days.

It was mid-afternoon by the time we got to Ranchi, but Sister Bernadette still seemed very keen to take me to see how the poor lived there. These divine sisters seemed to love showing me the lot of India's poor. This is partly because it's usually the poor who they mix with. It would have been rather nice, though, just for once to have visited India's rich - the high castes, the elite, the rich Hindus - to have seen their beautiful homes and see how the other half lives. When one thinks of India one tends to call to mind a country in the Third World with subjects living in dreadful squalor. But, believe me, there are many thousands of rich people in India. Not just rich, but super-rich people who are millionaires several times over. I automatically thought of the fat cats, making their millions off the backs of the poor. How can people live in the most beautiful mansions imaginable, some even in palaces, and not notice the degradation around them? I'd love to have made their acquaintance and visited the sheer splendour of their luxurious homes, where they would entertain guests in lavish style. Their plush life would be a world away from that of the destitute poor. But it's not a world away. In reality, just beyond their high walls and iron security gates, India's poor are starving. So it's probably just as well I didn't visit them. How can they justify their film star homes when their countrymen live in rat holes and in the most unbelievable conditions it's ever been my misfortune to see?

But, to continue with my last whole day in Ranchi, Sister Bernadette took me to a little hut just off the main road going into the town which was home to a woman and her three children. This turned out to be a particularly sad case where, several years ago, the woman's husband had just upped and left, abandoning his wife to bring up the children alone. The situation gave her many problems, not least, of course, financial ones. How could she manage? It's bad enough in England when this happens, but in India it's considerably worse, with no welfare payments whatsoever. Evidently Sister Bernadette had told her I was coming to see her and her family, and she had gone to great lengths to prepare a meal for me, an English meal, I might add, which I much appreciated. Her children were a boy of 12 and two daughters aged 10 and 8. Their home was spotlessly clean and the children's manners were impeccable. The son played cricket, which naturally interested me, and he took my breath away by saying his ambition was to be an airline pilot.

The family spoke in Hindi, translated into English for me by Sister Bernadette. I think the mother must have had a part-time job somewhere because she couldn't have managed bringing up three children alone with no money coming in. I had to admire the son who wanted to be an airline pilot. Ambition is a fine thing. It's driven us all on, I'm sure, to achieving certain things in our lives. But out in India it's different. There's the caste system. Albina Kujur has partly beaten it, but she will always remain lower caste. That boy's dream of becoming an airline pilot may well, therefore, go unfulfilled. If he could achieve it, I really would believe that India was prepared for change. For someone like myself, it's only on visiting India and seeing the horrors of the caste system that one realises that the weight of India's history and tradition makes it virtually impossible to change things. Of course, it's not impossible to change, if India really wants to. Would the rich of India be prepared, perhaps, to sacrifice that lavish lifestyle for change? The rich control the poor in India, so one day perhaps a Nelson Mandela will be born in the slums of Calcutta and will demand change. What that man did in South Africa was nothing short of incredible. So if South Africa can change from apartheid, why can't India change its caste system? Could that be achieved in India today? At present, I think, it's impossible. The rich Hindus would bitterly resent any change. They certainly wouldn't give up their lifestyle. But one never knows. I had begun to wonder whether South Africa would ever change from the evils of apartheid, but it did, so nothing's impossible.

After being in that little hut a good three hours, Sister Bernadette took me, by ambulance again, to the Ursuline convent school in the district of Hasag, which is still part of Ranchi. Sister Bernadette had worked at this school many times over the years and as usual I was introduced to many of the staff. One sister told me she had met me before. She was one of the teachers at the Lohardaga college when Albina had been a pupil there. She also came from Tongo village, so, she said, she felt close to Albina. She had even travelled with her to Bihar Sharif for that interview. So here I was again thanking an Ursuline sister for what she'd done for Albina. In no time I was being entertained by orphans from this school - 200 children singing for my pleasure. For the umpteenth time I was garlanded with flowers. I've certainly got a good rapport with Indian school children and wherever I've been at those convent schools I've received a glorious welcome. Usually I've also known a member of the school's staff. At the Lohardaga college I knew a lot of the sisters and it's the same wherever I've been in India. I've always known someone. Partly this is because I visited the schools on my last trip. It is also partly because the sisters have read my book. When it was first published I sent several copies to Sister Bernadette at Tongo. She distributed them to certain sisters in various parts of South Bihar. I had even sent one to Sister Albina Dunguong, who had moved to north east India, in that isolated area near China. So, not surprisingly, some of the sisters knew of me through reading my book. It has travelled somewhat.

On that last evening in Bihar I went with Sister Bernadette into Ranchi to make a telephone call to her brother, Dr Tete, in New Delhi. I had to tell him I couldn't get involved with helping to raise money for the new hospital that was so desperately needed in South Bihar. I could sense his disappointment and I must admit I felt quite guilty. I felt I'd let him down. In fact, I felt I'd let many people down, particularly the people of the village of Gotra. But I hadn't promised anyone I'd help with this hospital, so why feel this guilt? It was because there was just nothing I could do about the situation. Part of me wanted to help, but I couldn't possibly get involved in two ventures at the same time. My allegiance to the Tongo school must come first, I told him. Sister Bernadette and her brother had expected an awful lot from me. How on earth was I going to raise

£100,000? Where does one start in a situation like that? In that field that day at Gotra I had wanted a dream to come true for those people. Sister Bernadette had told me they would get no help from the Indian government for the hospital. I remember asking why the rich Hindus couldn't help the poor. She quickly told me they could expect no help from that quarter.

"The rich have never helped the poor yet. It would be a waste of time even asking them," she said with a shrug of her shoulders. I think again of India's mega-rich. There must be a Good Samaritan out there somewhere. Surely there are rich Hindus who help the poor. I cannot believe that all those people can go about their lives and not be affected by the poor people of their own country dying through lack of medical attention. One thing I do know for sure is that however much wealth we have in this world, when we go to the great beyond we certainly can't take it with us. Ashes to ashes, dust to dust. Need I say more?

At the Ranchi convent school I was given the same bedroom as five years ago. I did a quick inspection of the mosquito net covering my bed for any small holes there might be in it. I was getting somewhat fed up being bitten by the blessed insects. That evening I looked back on my two weeks in India. Once again the time had been action-packed from start to finish. The sheer excitement of being in India leaves me on a permanent high. I just can't get enough of the country. The highlight of that last day was surely meeting Sister Angeline again. "It's a miracle," she had told me. Seeing her again was proof to me that miracles do happen.

But also that evening the old pre-flight nerves were beginning to eat into me as another dreaded plane trip began to draw ever closer. My flight would be leaving Ranchi for Calcutta the following afternoon. But what I didn't know at the time, and, with hindsight, perhaps that was just as well, was the further excitement awaiting me - a real cliffhanger. I could quite probably have done without such excitement, but, looking back, I wouldn't have missed it. This experience would broaden my experience yet again on a subject I'd read much about and seen a lot of on TV. Indian travel is precarious to say the least. At times it's catastrophic and I was to be part of something that answered to that description as I and more than 1,000 people embarked on a train passage to Calcutta.

Chapter Ten

A Train Passage to Calcutta

"Now, Papa, shall I get married?" said Albina Kujur on that last morning that I was with her at the Ranchi convent school. She had travelled through the night by bus from Bihar Sharif to be with me and see me off from the airport later that afternoon. She had arrived at nine o'clock that morning and was most anxious to discuss this question with me. She had written to me about six months previously, saying she had met a nice boy from New Delhi and asking not only for my opinion but also my permission so she could marry. We had raised this subject when I had arrived in Bihar just over a week before. Readers might find it difficult to understand why a young lady from the Indian countryside should ask for my permission to get married, but because I had sponsored her from the age of 11 she felt she had to get my approval. Even her parents had told her to get my permission. I know that if I'd said no she would never have brought the subject up again, but, in all honesty, who was I to disapprove? I asked her if she loved him and she told me she did. I enquired about what he did for a living and was told he was desperate for work but unfortunately could only get part-time jobs.

"He wants very much to marry me, but he has no regular job. I won't get married if you don't want me to," Albina had said. How could I possibly advise her - or anyone, come to that - about whether she should get married? Marriage is without doubt one of the biggest decisions we make in our lives. I was certainly no marriage counsellor, either. She looked on me as a second father. Whatever I'd have said she would have agreed to. She was 27 years of age and the look in her eyes told me she was pleading with me for help. Her marriage to this boy would not be the traditional arranged variety but a marriage based on love. Surely, therefore, it stood a chance. A couple in England meet, fall in love and marry. What could be simpler? But this was not England, it was India and I just didn't know how to advise her.

As we talked that morning, all sorts of thoughts were coming into my head. What happens if, after the marriage, Albina's husband can't find work? It would mean her 'keeping' him. Also, let's say that after marriage she becomes pregnant and her husband is still out of work. What then? How would they manage if she continued to have children? With no child benefits in India, how would they survive? It could be that she might never teach again. All that education she had received and the four years at the training college would be wasted. I could see lots of complications and the last thing I wanted for her was to be unhappy. She had worked so very hard to reach this school teaching position and it could all be thrown away. I knew she absolutely loved teaching.

"Think long and hard about what you really want in your life," I remember saying. I was her Papa, as she called me, and I'd really tried to give her the correct advice. But what was the correct advice in that situation? She could marry, have lots of children and be utterly miserable. What I do know from seeing her again this second time is that her teaching job gives her such pleasure and contentment that it shines through in her personality. I don't believe she can realise just how lucky she has been in her life. She must look at her friends in Tongo, most of them with children, and think that they could never become what she has become. And her contentment gives her that confidence that was lacking before. Five years ago she had been quite shy at times, but not any more. This was very noticeable when she was with her family and friends and the Ursuline sisters. She is indeed a confident young lady. But I'd been placed in an awkward position. She had asked for my advice, but how could I possibly advise a country girl from India about marriage, and also what right had I to stand in her way whatever path she chose? Marriage is a gamble for us all, but in Albina's case even more so. She could marry, have many children and live exactly the same life her parents and millions of others out in the countryside had lived, or she could forsake marriage, remain a school teacher and continue with something she obviously found fulfilling. With the education she has received, she has become a somebody in India. Not much, mind you, but a somebody nevertheless. She had desperately wanted my opinion, but unfortunately I hadn't been much help.

Also that morning, John Kujur, Albina's brother, and his wife and two young daughters came to say goodbye. He is most unhappy in his job. "No prospects," he kept telling me. He is a waiter in a hotel and he also told me his pay was so poor that he could hardly keep his wife and children. He actually speaks very good English and comes across as quite an intelligent person, who, given the chance, could have made something of himself. But, like millions of his countrymen, he is in a dead-end job, though at least he is working so he does at least have that to be thankful for. After saying goodbye to him and his wife, Sister Bernadette insisted I accompany her to the chapel.

"We must pray that you have a good flight home," she said. As we came away from the chapel after being inside for about 10 minutes, she said: "I'm happier now because I know you will get home safely."

"How can you say that?" I asked.

"You will see. Have no fear, you will arrive home safely," she repeated. With several of the sisters praying in that chapel for my safe return it did cross my mind that I might have a fair chance of making it.

I said goodbye to some of the resident Ursuline sisters at the convent and climbed aboard the ambulance again for the short journey to Ranchi Airport. With Albina to see me off were Sister Margaret Mary, Sister Scholastica, Sister Michael, Sister Vianney and Sister Bernadette. What a sendoff I'd be getting from six people who had looked after me so very well. Ranchi, at one time the hill station of the summer retreat of the British, is easily the most overcrowded of all the towns and cities I've been to in India. To see the sheer mass of human bodies in those streets takes one's breath away. There are light industrial companies in the town, so there is work there. There is also the biggest mental asylum in all India. Being a hill station at an altitude of 2,135 feet, Ranchi has a most pleasant climate compared with some other areas of Bihar. What it also has, of course, is the sacred cow. These animals wander the streets at will and all over India one never escapes the sacred cow of Hinduism. Under no circumstances is it permitted to harm them and their charmed life comes in part from their working role in the countryside. They are also marvellously mild-mannered and it is said they would never attack you. They gobble up literally everything they come across in those dirty streets. I've even seen them eating pieces of rotten wood. The cows seem to be oblivious to any noise around them and when a Westerner goes to India for the first time, probably the first thing they will notice is the cows and bulls roaming the streets. The fun starts when they cross a busy road. With magnificent impertinence they will stroll in front of any approaching vehicle, often leaving the driver up in arms with rage, but when you are regarded as a God, you must be tolerated - even if you are an animal. Not so many years ago in India, one could face the death penalty for killing a cow and even now the punishment could be a prison term. I even had the feeling those sacred cows actually knew how important they were. With their magnificent bearing they seem to control those Indian streets.

Also there to see me off at the airport, where my flight to Calcutta was scheduled for 4.10pm, was the lady and her three children who Sister Bernadette had taken me to see the day before - so there was quite a gathering there. As I sat in the airport lounge I just hoped my flight would run smoothly, with no more complications. Surely I'd had enough disruptions with my two previous flights. Surely I'd have no problems with any flight from now on. By the law of averages I should be OK... but, sure enough, over the Tannoy came the announcement that my flight to Calcutta had been cancelled, just like that. I refused to believe it could happen again. Three flights I had booked and I'd had trouble with every one. I knew Indian Airlines were unreliable at times, but this was ridiculous. Panic then set in. What was I to do? There were no flights to Calcutta for four days and I had to get there to catch my flight back to Heathrow at 9.15pm next day. I was in a terrible predicament. All my friends who had waited with me were equally devastated as I contemplated exactly how I was to get to Calcutta.

In that airport lounge I'd got talking to two Catholic priests, one Belgian, the other Dutch. They were as desperate as I was to get to Calcutta because like me they had flights to catch the next day. They asked me if I was interested in going with them on a sleeper train to Calcutta. Apparently, one left from Ranchi every evening. I definitely was interested and the three of us made enquiries at the airport reception desk. The airport officials, who had been very apologetic about the cancelled flight, were most sympathetic to our cause and we were eventually told we had been booked onto this overnight sleeper. We were then taken to a hotel in Ranchi, where a meal had been provided by the airline for the passengers of the flight that never was. My group of friends were also allowed into this very attractive hotel and after the meal we sat around talking as we waited for my 8.30pm night journey by rail to Calcutta.

While sitting in that excellent hotel it crossed my mind that Albina might be asked to leave. Being from a low caste she wouldn't normally be allowed in, but fortunately nobody said anything. Eventually, after about two hours, it was time to get to Ranchi railway station. As my place on the train had been booked, along with the priests, there was no immediate rush, but from previous experience I knew it was a good idea to get there in good time just in case the train left early. One can never be sure in India. The short walk to the station took only a few minutes, but the streets of Ranchi looked busier that ever. All the shops were open and crowds of people were swamping the pavements. Where do they all come from, I asked myself continually. Walking to the station with the sisters, Albina and the two priests, it struck me that Ranchi would not be the ideal place for a single white person to walk about on their own, particularly at night. Anything could happen. Like the other towns I visited, one doesn't see white people and one can feel vulnerable, believe me. But I was actually looking forward to this 10-hour train journey through the night. Indian railways cover 62,000 km, by far the biggest network in Asia, and the fourth largest in the world. This was to be a new experience for me in my travels through the sub-continent. It was to be a nostalgic return to the great days of steam. On making it to the station we discovered crowds gathered outside. Why so many people, I thought. Surely they didn't all expect to catch the train. Even before we got on the platform we had to push through the crowds congregating outside.

Once on the platform I noticed the untouchables. A little crowd of them were huddled together, shunned as usual by all. They are below the lowest caste, ostracised by everyone, despised throughout India. Untouchable means just that - not to be touched. Even the lower caste would cross the road rather than walk by an untouchable. They are treated like outcasts. The untouchables are members of the lowest class in India, the lowest of the four main castes. That great man of peace Mahatma Gandhi, who could see the great injustice of the untouchables' position, even went so far as to describe them as the children of God. He was so appalled by the way they were treated. They really are outcasts from all society. Gandhi actually wanted to improve their lives, but the Hindus wouldn't tolerate that, so the untouchables would always remain untouchable, not to be touched by anyone. What a dreadful life they live. If they are lucky enough to find work it's usually one of the demeaning jobs like picking human and animal excrement off India's dirty streets. India certainly does not have anything to be proud of in the way it treats its untouchables.

Once the train I was about to catch had left that railway station the untouchables and the poor of Ranchi would bed down there for the night. Their skeleton-like figures would have an old blanket or sack pulled over them to protect their shockingly thin bodies from the cold at night. Literally hundreds of Ranchi's poor would be sleeping rough on the platform, but those old sacks wouldn't necessarily be for protection just from the cold, but also from rats. Yes, rats again. Swarms of them. I remember only about a year ago reading in an English newspaper that New Delhi, which has a population of 12 million people, has at least five rats for every one person, so it doesn't take a great mathematician to work out that there are millions upon millions of rats in that city. I'm reminded as I write of a lady who heard me speak about India. She told me that the hotel she stayed at on a visit to India was right opposite a railway station. Every night hundreds of the poor people in the town where she was staying would sleep rough in that station, with just an old sack pulled over them. From her bedroom window every evening she would look on in amazement as rats came out of their holes and descended on the platform. She said hundreds of rats, maybe thousands, were scurrying all over those sacks, trying to get to the people underneath. The very thought is enough to make you shiver, isn't it? It's widely known in these Indian towns and cities that the destitute poor are being bitten and nibbled repeatedly by hordes of rats. The poor of India are to be found every night huddled together in railway and bus stations. At least there they get protection from the rain, particularly important during the monsoon season. It's no wonder that India is a rat-infested country. It is alive with them. The rate at which they breed must be gigantic. Every night the poor survive in horrific conditions to see the breaking of another day, another day of sheer misery, the misery of living through and surviving somehow to another day which for us in the West would be a nightmare. With no food or water they are in a hopeless situation and, if they are lucky, death might come as some sort of release.

Imagine coming out of a football match in England where you are shoulder to shoulder with crowds of people, and in order to get to where you want to go you are pushing and shoving your way through. That's how it seemed on Ranchi railway station that evening. The general buzz and excitement of being on that station made me feel like I was about to start a great adventure, a journey into the unknown. The feeling I was getting was quite exceptional. In fact, it was exhilarating. One couldn't help but be caught up by the atmosphere of that station. It felt as though something major was about to happen. But in many respects it had also left me in a nervous state, wondering what this train journey was going to be like. It was quite an experience being on that station that evening with so many people, but I was having awful problems with my suitcase and cursing my friend David's very name. He had asked me to bring back from India the very heaviest piece of wood I could possibly find. He wanted to make some table fruit bowls from real Indian wood, the heavier the better, he'd said. After much searching and help from the sisters at Tongo, a really heavy piece of Indian wood was duly found. Even the part-time gardeners at Tongo had found great difficulty hand-sawing through it. The wood was so tough it had taken hours to saw and now it was taking up half my suitcase. I seemed to be hauling this heavy piece of wood all the way round Ranchi station. That's why my suitcase was so heavy, so heavy in fact that I feared it might split open. I could scarcely contemplate all my personal belongings being scattered all over that station and the thought of me diving under thousands of legs searching for what I'd lost scared me to death.

With my back not quite fully recovered I had struggled repeatedly with my suitcase. As women do a lot of the heavy work in India it would have been quite acceptable for Albina to have been carrying it. At times she was literally trying to pull it away from me in her determination to carry it, but I was equally determined not to let her have it. As I've said before, she is certainly not one of the strongest people and I couldn't possibly allow her to take it. Then panic set in among the crowds on that station platform. I'd suddenly lost everyone. There were no familiar faces, just masses of unfamiliar ones I'd never set eyes on in my life. I had been jostled and pushed in so many directions that I was completely on my own. One can easily panic among such crowds. Then, as quickly as I'd lost my friends I was reunited with them again. From then on I stuck to them like glue. I couldn't afford to lose them again. On arriving at one end of the platform, which seemed to take forever, we were told that to board the train with my ticket we would have to be at the other end. So, back through those crowds again, which as you can imagine was quite punishing. With my heavy suitcase I'd found it most exhausting. Then the excitement reached fever pitch when, above all the noise on that station, the train could be heard approaching. The people in the middle of the platform, where the crowd was at its thickest, seemed to surge forwards. They were being carried by the sheer mass of humanity. Surely someone would fall and be trampled. Also, I might add, the lighting on that platform was very poor indeed. Fortunately, as my compartment was booked, there was no need for the priests and I to move. We just stood there, taking in the spectacle before us. The determined look on the faces of some of the people on that platform said that no way were they going to miss out on boarding that train. And then, in semi-darkness, the great monster of a steam engine appeared from out of the night outside the station. In such poor light it had a ghostly look about it. It appeared, shrouded in billowing smoke, and amid the chuffing of its engine and the clanging of its wheels it ground to a halt. That giant engine, a relic of the imperial British Raj, had a distinctly Made in Britain look to it.

People started clamouring to get on board and even more of them surged forwards. Once the train was in the station the lighting appeared to get better and the priests and I found our carriage the end of a row of 10. With much difficulty, and help from a railway guard, I managed to get my suitcase on board. Once I'd found the compartment I left the suitcase with the priests and quickly rejoined my friends on the platform. Seeing those crowds of people clamouring to get on board that train is something I'll never forget. How many passengers were scampering on board I'll never know. The train was obviously going to be overloaded. I'd seen pictures on TV of overcrowded trains in India and I was going to be part of one such situation for real.

As I stood on the platform with Albina and the sisters, Sister Sarita made an appearance, having travelled from Tongo that afternoon. She had found us with difficulty, but she had managed it and that made it six Ursuline sisters on the platform to see me off. While I was talking to them the whistle was blown. The train was about to go. After giving each sister and Albina a hug it was up the steps and onto the carriage. I opened the window and, leaning through, I began chatting to them. I waited for the train to move, but nothing happened.

The excitement on that platform was intense. In fact, the whole atmosphere was electric, everyone on tenter-hooks waiting for the great train to move. By this time black smoke was billowing from the engine's funnel, seemingly making the platform even darker. Why wasn't the train moving, people seemed to be asking. After a few minutes I opened the carriage door and rejoined my friends, but, as I stood on the platform the whistle rang out once more, so after more hugs and kisses I was back up the steps and into the carriage. I leaned out of the window again, and again nothing happened. Further down the platform the train seemed to be spluttering into action, but it couldn't get moving. Perhaps there were too many people on board, I thought. Once more I joined my friends, only for the guard to blow his whistle for the third time, prompting another round of hugs and kisses and another leap back to the carriage. This was it, I thought, third time lucky. The train would definitely be moving this time. But alas nothing happened. I rejoined the sisters. Everyone, both on the platform and aboard the train, was getting increasingly frustrated at the complete lack of movement. The procedure of me jumping on and off the train must have happened half a dozen times. This was typical India. Whether it's rail travel or airline flights, nothing goes on time. I decided, finally, to stay on the platform until I saw the train actually moving. After probably about eight blows of the whistle the train did finally begin to move amid much chuffing, spluttering and puffing. Yes, believe it or not, the train was moving at last. I hugged all the sisters one last time. I'm sure those Divine Sisters have never been kissed so much in all their lives. After also holding Albina one last time I jumped aboard and, with shouting and waving all around, leant out of the carriage door's window. The build-up of smoke and steam was intense as the train started to pull out of Ranchi station.

I can remember Albina's last words to me despite all the noise on that platform: "Goodbye, Papa. Take care," she said. The sisters were shouting "Goodbye, Mr Brian," as chaos reigned. Amid the din I could hear the great iron, British-built, locomotive steam engine spluttering and chuffing again and once more its massive wheels were clanging. This vast relic from the days of the British Raj was finally on the move, with passengers leaning out of the windows, waving and bellowing their goodbyes while hundreds waved back furiously from the platform. The scene might have been not unlike that on the dockside as the Titanic set off on its maiden voyage across the Atlantic. The train was making a heck of a noise as it struggled to pick up speed. I was still leaning out of the window of my carriage door and waving like mad. Gradually, the train began to move more quickly and I continued to think it must be very overloaded. I then did something really stupid. I opened the carriage door and, with my left hand gripping a handrail, I was able to hang right out of that carriage while continuing to wave furiously with my right hand. Everyone aboard that train and on the platform seemed to be waving someone off and as I hung out of the carriage door, those hundreds on the platform seemed to be getting smaller. The sisters' uniforms were gradually receding. As the speed increased, my special group of friends was disappearing before my very eyes. Amid so much smoke and steam I had trouble seeing them at all, and then a final puff of smog blocked my view and that was it. They had gone and as the train pulled into the darkness of the night I felt numb. No words can really describe how I felt at that time. If I never set eyes on Albina or the sisters again I will never forget those final dramatic minutes. It really was the most heartbreaking farewell and if I live to be 100 I will never forget it.

The sadness I felt as the train left Ranchi made me so despondent and gave me a feeling of great loneliness. I was on my own once more and I was reluctant to join the two priests in my compartment. I would have been poor company for anyone. All I wanted was to get home as quickly as possible. That last goodbye made me homesick. I felt so dreadfully homesick. England was my home and I couldn't wait to get there.

On the carriage I quickly recognised several of the passengers who, like me, had been stranded at Ranchi Airport. All of them were Europeans, who had wanted to get to Calcutta at the earliest opportunity. After about half an hour of standing about in the corridor I finally went into my compartment. I couldn't hang around any longer because it would have been rude not to have joined the two priests. They had been so helpful to me, doing all the running round to get me my rail tickets. Once in the compartment I was still feeling really quite subdued. I had experienced the same kind of feeling when I'd said farewell to Albina and the sisters five years earlier at Ranchi Airport. Twice in my life I had said goodbye to them and twice I'd been left thoroughly miserable, but I had to put it all to one side and concentrate on the rail journey before me. Clickety-clack, clickety-clack came the noise from the carriage wheels on the railway lines. I could hear the giant steam engine chuffing and throwing out smoke as it left the state of Bihar. It gave me some sort of comfort that the train was probably built in Britain. At the turn of the century, trains brought into India would have been either British or, to a lesser extent,

American. When the British Raj ruled India, those engines would have used a spider's web of railway lines right through the whole subcontinent. In today's India, 7,000 passenger trains are in daily use, carrying 10.5 million people who use more than 7,000 stations. This giant railway system also employs more than 1.6 million people, making it easily the world's largest in terms of manpower.

Once in the compartment I immediately noticed there was an additional passenger. This man of about 60 greeted me very sociably as I sat down, saying he was a German businessman travelling to Calcutta to catch a plane to Australia the next day. So, with the two priests there too, I seemed to be in good company. On my train journey to Calcutta I had a Belgian, a Dutchman and a German for company and luckily for me all the conversation was in English, with all three of my fellow passengers having a good command of the language. So, with four different nationalities in the same compartment, guess what we got talking about? No, not European football, but the European Union. It proved most interesting, with the German doing most of the talking. I happened to mention that I was a bit of a Euro-sceptic. They looked puzzled and I could see they couldn't understand what I meant. To put it simply, I told them, I didn't agree with everything going on in the EU.

"Great Britain will lose its identity. Decisions are being made in Brussels which will have a lasting effect and we shan't need our Parliament soon," I remember saying. The Dutchman nodded in agreement. "But to make it work we must all come together as one," he said.

"It's hardly Great Britain any more, is it?" said the German, repeating after a pause: "I mean it's hardly great, is it?" I felt I was being pushed into a corner. I was hardly going to agree with him. I was just about to reply when the German surprised me by saying: "It couldn't have been easy for Britain to join the Common Market because of its great history. Look what your country has achieved throughout the world. Look at the great British Empire, which at one time was spread across the globe. Britain has had immense influence in so many countries." I looked more closely at this German, who appeared to be saying everything I'd ever wanted to hear about my country. He understood what a great step it had been for Britain to join what was then the Common Market. He was so sympathetic to our cause. "For your country, which not so many years ago was such a world power, it must have been very difficult to become just an ordinary member of the Common Market," he said.

I was warming to this man by the second. He was talking such a lot of good sense. This had surprised me because when he had started talking about Britain not being great any more I'd thought he was taking the mickey. But no, I had been wrong. The two priests had joined in lively conversation, saying Europe had many problems. Again the German spoke and we all listened.

"Germany has enormous problems, a tremendous level of unemployment and other internal troubles which are eating away at the government. And of course there is the East Germany situation. Germany probably has more problems than your country," he said looking at me.

"Although I'm a Euro-sceptic I realise we must work together. I certainly wouldn't want my country to leave the European Union. Besides, if the existence of the EU means a Europe forever free of wars it must be a good thing," I replied.

The two priests couldn't have agreed more with that last remark. The German also nodded. He of all people would know of the horrors of war.

"No, never again. Never," he said. The four of us had indulged in quite a stimulating conversation. Four nationalities thrown together on a train through the very heart of the Indian countryside at night on our train passage to Calcutta.

Our conversation was broken as the guard came to check our rail tickets. I asked him how many people were on board. He smiled and said 875. One of the priests asked if that was the official number. He seemed to shrug his shoulders and appeared not to want to know. I'd asked the question because, having seen that packed railway station at Ranchi, I was fairly confident there were more than 875 people on board. Maybe people were sitting on the carriage roofs or hanging on to window ledges, as they were in the many TV pictures I have seen of overcrowded trains in India. Perhaps by shrugging his shoulders the guard meant he hadn't a clue how many people there were on board. The people I saw clamouring on those carriages gave me the idea that there must be at least 1,200 people on board. This was not one of the luxury passenger trains frequently seen on the Indian railways, but just an ordinary one. I well remember when, on my last visit to India, I took a train from New Delhi to Agra to see the Taj Mahal. That really was one of the most luxurious 1st class passenger trains in the whole of the Indian railway network. Breakfast was served and one generally had the feeling of travelling in style, but the Indian tourist authorities would have to lay on such transport for all the tourists coming to New Delhi and journeying on to the Taj Mahal. In contrast, the train to Calcutta that I was on that night was certainly not luxurious. Our compartment was very ordinary indeed, with just four berths. But I had the feeling we were lucky. I dreaded to think how comfortable or uncomfortable some of the other carriages were. How does one sleep standing up? Some of the passengers would undoubtedly have been doing just that in their grossly overcrowded carriages. Our compartment was definitely not luxurious, but our conditions were 10 times better than in most of the other passenger carriages on that night sleeper.

By 11pm the priests decided it was time for bed. The bunks were made up and my continental friends and I settled down for a night's sleep. While lying on my bunk bed above the German, who incidentally seemed to be off to sleep in no time, I knew I was in for yet another poor night's sleep. The racket caused by the wheels rattling on the tracks was obviously going to continue all night. Clickety-clack, clickety-clack, came the incessant noise. Naturally, it kept me awake. And to make matters worse, every half an hour the train would come to a grinding halt. Since I've been home I've looked at a map and, drawing a straight line between Ranchi and Calcutta, I worked out that the distance was 250 miles. But in reality it is very much longer. The track varies a great deal and it is hardly straight. The train stopped at small villages off the main route, suggesting to me that the distance was very much longer than the as-the-crow-flies mileage. Putting the distances between villages into my calculations I arrived at a total of 350 miles between Ranchi and Calcutta. That night it seemed more like 1,000. It seemed that just as the train had pulled out of one station it was drawing into the next, perhaps some outpost miles from anywhere. At most stops there was the excitement of people noisily getting on and off. The train seemed to be as old as the hills, and every time it pulled away it would cough and splutter to get going again. The great days of steam were well and truly with me that night as the hissing of the engine and its chuffing and puffing made sure there was no sleep for me. Whistles were forever blowing and I'm sure the train hardly got above 35 mph. Just as well, really, because being perched on that bunk bed made for a rickety, rocky ride. The carriage's constant swaying from side to side contributed further to making me long for the peace and quiet of my own bed, so desperate was I for sleep. While lying on that bunk bed I couldn't stop wondering where on earth we were going. I thought of the train going over broken-down bridges and through tunnels, swamps and paddy fields and heaven knows what else. Indian Railways have an appalling safety record. Many times over the years their trains have collided head-on and only a month after I returned home this happened in a tunnel, with 700 people killed. With the carriages so overcrowded it's little wonder the death tolls are so high.

Although my compartment had air conditioning it was hardly keeping me cool. The heat was quite stifling, even though it was November and one of the cooler times of the year. It made me think of what the heat in those carriages must be like in the summer months. In some carriages, the overcrowding would make the heat even more overpowering and suffocating, with passengers being squashed together. Also, my compartment wasn't too clean and I hate using pillows and blankets which may have been used before. After many hours lying awake on that bunk bed, I noticed the daylight starting to break as another day began. At 5am the sun was doing its best to come out. That day was to be my last in India. At that time, my plan on arrival in Calcutta was to make straight for the Kenilworth Hotel, hopefully get a room there and have a shower and a shave, grabbing some overdue sleep before making my way to Dum Dum Airport for my evening flight home.

At long last, after a night that had seemed like an eternity, the clickety-clack began to slow down and that meant the great steam engine was approaching Howrah Railway Station. As the train drew closer to Calcutta the scenery changed from the colourful brightness of the East Bengal countryside to the impoverished environment of the city's slums. On either side of the railway track there must have been thousands of bustees. The inhabitants were waking up to another day of gloom and depression. Thousands of people cram into those makeshift shacks. Having been to the City of Joy I knew exactly what the conditions were like there. As there were no toilets, the slum-dwellers could be seen relieving themselves at the side of the railway line and they were also seen queuing by the dozen to wash at a standpipe. How do they survive in these places? I'm sure if I saw 1,000 different slum areas I would still be taken by surprise, as if I'm seeing a slum for the very first time. I just cannot - and will never - understand how in the 20th century a good quarter of the world's population can live their lives in conditions so intolerable that we in the West would not subject our pets to. Surely this world of ours has made some progress since it began. Seeing what I saw that morning from that carriage window made me wonder, not for the first time, whether our world has in fact progressed at all.

About five minutes from Howrah Station the train ground to a halt and to my surprise dozens of boys of about the 12 to 14 age bracket were running over the tracks to board the train. Carriage doors were being pulled open and these lads scampered inside. In no time, one boy took my suitcase from my compartment and I went in hot pursuit. The German told me this was quite normal on Indian railways.

"He wants to carry your case for you," he said. Inside our carriage dozens of Indian boys had hold of a suitcase. The train started up again and we arrived at Howrah Station. The great locomotive, with thick smoke billowing from its funnel was chuffing and spluttering in clouds of steam as its huge wheels changed to an abrupt halt at the end of the 350-mile, 10-hour, journey. Panic then appeared to set in. People seemingly couldn't get off the train quick enough. Pandemonium then broke out with more pushing and shoving and such confusion that the scene was similar to the one in Ranchi when I had boarded the train. Instead of being in a hurry to get on the train, people seemed to be desperate to get off it. For a few seconds I lost the boy who had my suitcase balanced on his head, holding both ends with his hands. The case was so heavy that I was sure he would sink under the weight. His face was quite red.

"Taxi, taxi," he kept shouting. "You follow," he said. It was probably the only English he knew. I had just about managed to say goodbye to my three fellow passengers, but I never saw them again on that station.

Pandemonium is a good word to describe Howrah Station, which is almost a city in itself. There is such a buzz generated by people rushing to and from the platforms either to catch trains or having disembarked. The station is not far from the slum area close to the River Houghly that I'd visited just over a week earlier. There seems to be a permanent contingent of slum-dwellers either cooking over their little stoves, sleeping or begging. Small traders also sell their wares amid the hustle and bustle of blaring loud-speakers and old steam engines shunting and chuffing and smoke and steam billowing all over the station. The station was surprisingly clean and I thought it was an improvement on Ranchi Station. The boy who had taken my oh-so-heavy case had earned a good tip, which was of course why he had scampered on to my carriage in the first place. He also took me to where I could catch a taxi and once out of that huge station it felt good to be in Calcutta again. What a difference to when I'd first arrived in that city just under two weeks before. That Sunday morning I'd got a spring in my step and a good-to-be-alive feeling. It felt really wonderful to be in the sunshine of Calcutta. Looking back on that train journey through the night I wouldn't have missed it for anything. Seeing another aspect of Indian life had broadened my knowledge of the country yet again. I can only describe travel on Indian railways as precarious and chaotic because, lying on that bunk bed at 3am on a rickety old banger of a train with the carriage swaying so much that I feared it might come off the rails, I had begun to wonder what I'd let myself in for as we travelled through the wilds of the Indian countryside. So, standing in the sunshine in Calcutta, it was absolutely marvellous to be there, slums and all.

Chapter Eleven

Survival on the Streets

"Where have you been, Mr Brian? We were expecting you yesterday," said one of the assistant managers as I walked into the Kenilworth Hotel at 7.30 that Sunday morning in Calcutta. I told him about the last-minute cancellation of my Ranchi flight and he shook his head, muttering something about Indian Airways. After offering my apologies I was offered a room for a few hours. I had to smile to myself, as throughout my travels I'd always been called Mr Brian. Very rarely had my surname been used. Even the bell captain of that magnificent hotel always referred to me as Mr Brian. I couldn't help smiling to myself again as the bell captain ordered two porters to carry my suitcase. Seeing them both struggling with it was really funny. The looks they were giving me said 'what on earth have you got in here?' I wondered how that young boy at Howrah Station had managed to carry it. My smiles turned to laughter when, on arrival at my room, the porters lifted my case onto a small table, which promptly collapsed into a heap of wood on the carpet. The look the porters gave me at that point told me they didn't know whether to laugh or cry. Breaking a small table may have been a sackable offence in that hotel for all I knew and maybe their jobs were threatened, but that suitcase was certainly heavy and the table shattering under the weight wasn't their fault. I only hope my friend David appreciates the problems that case was causing.

After a lovely hot shower and shave (I must confess, a shower or bath was something I really did miss at Tongo) it was time for some sleep. On a most comfortable bed and in a room containing mod cons like air conditioning I would hopefully sleep at last. With my flight not due until that evening I was hoping for many hours' sleep. But could I sleep? No way. I was desperate for sleep, but I just couldn't get it. I don't think I'd completely recovered from the excitement of that train journey, so eventually I decided to get up and look around Calcutta again, though only in the vicinity of the hotel. One thing that continues to fascinate me about Indian cities is that one minute one can be in the most beautiful hotel possible, while the next one can be amid the squalor of the filthiest streets. Walking out of hotels to find the poverty, misery and starvation all around repeatedly surprised me. As soon as I was on the streets outside that hotel, the beggars were waiting. They obviously thought this white man who was able to stay in such splendour had pots of money. The reason I was able to stay in such a hotel was that all hotels in India are cheap compared to British ones. So, I hadn't got pots of money, but the beggars weren't to know that, and I was forever being pestered. Once out in the sunshine I had to see another of my favourite places in Calcutta, only about 10 minutes' walk from the hotel. I just had to have one final look at St. Paul's Cathedral.

Calcutta is only about 300 years old. Originally it was a village called Kalikata. Because of its rapid growth, Calcutta, like many cities worldwide, has changed over the years. Many new buildings had sprung up even in the five years since I had last been there. It is either a city one will visit time and again, or a place that, having experienced once, one will never want to see again. Seeing Calcutta can be very upsetting. It forces one to examine all notions of human potential and it really is an overpowering experience. Calcutta's character has been well and truly shaped by the British Raj. Great buildings reach for the sky. One of them is the imposing, Gothic, St. Paul's Cathedral, built between 1839 and 1847. It stands near the Victoria Memorial Hall and was by all accounts the first cathedral to be built in the British Empire. The tower was modelled on Canterbury Cathedral. The reason I love visiting this cathedral is its architecture and classical structure. There is not just a little bit, but a large slice of Britain in that cathedral. I could have stayed there for hours amid the kind of peace and tranquillity one just does not find anywhere other than in churches and cathedrals. The main reason for visiting that cathedral, though, was that it was Remembrance Sunday. Unfortunately the main service had ended before I arrived, but I was pleased to discover that Remembrance Sunday is not forgotten in India, and the expatriates, those people who support their country so vigorously while living abroad, are working hard to keep that cathedral open.

The ex-pats, or should I say Anglicans, in Calcutta have achieved their goal by merging with other major non-Catholic denominations to form the Churches of North India. I'm sure that during the days of the Raj that cathedral would have been a hive of activity, with military services and great parades with bands going on all around. With all the place's history and heritage, not to mention beauty, it would be an absolute tragedy if through lack of support it had to close down, or, even worse, be demolished. That could well happen if the ex-pats die off, which they undoubtedly will, or return to England. That cathedral could well reach a crisis, with Christians making up less than five per cent of the Indian population. It is difficult to see the 85 per cent who are Hindu having any reason to visit the building, so it is really up to the Anglicans to preserve it. While in the cathedral I had got talking to an English lady who had lived in Calcutta for 47 years, and her love for the cathedral was immense. It was her little England and it was vital to her that it remained open. But attendances are dwindling and congregations are declining. There are other Anglican churches in the city. The two I'd visited when last there were St. John's and St. Andrew's, but it was St. Paul's Cathedral that had left such an impression on me. It is imperative for the memory of the British Empire that the cathedral and those churches remain open, but my fear is that one day they will be pulled down, for the simple reason that the congregations will be non-existent. May the ex-pats live on in Calcutta, if only to prevent that beautiful cathedral and those churches from disappearing.

Walking back to the hotel, I had to cross a very busy road. So busy is it that you take your life in your hands to cross it. Admittedly there are traffic lights, but they do not give a feeling of total security as one crosses with extreme nervousness past steaming hot vehicles and often impatient drivers, with the air thick with fumes and the smell of burnt oil caused by the constant revving of engines. Amidst all this smog, the rickshaw pullers weave in and out of the traffic. Literally thousands of them are to be seen all over the city, coughing up blood in order to deliver their passengers. These rickshaw pullers are often referred to as human horses with their chariots of fire. In their bare feet they are running all over Calcutta. I doubt if any of them live past 40. They must die of exhaustion well before then. Their terribly thin bodies are skin and bones with extremely pronounced rib cages. I've never seen such shockingly ill people in all my life. They might have three or even more passengers aboard as they struggle to pull their rickshaws. It is the deadly exhaust fumes which cause them to cough up blood. The local mafia controls all rickshaw pullers in the city and nearly all their hard-earned money is handed over to these people, who are absolutely ruthless towards them. Nobody can be a rickshaw puller unless they are under mafia control. They are left with barely enough money to support a family and if they should utter so much as a word of protest about their miserly wages they face being beaten up and banned from the streets forever. The human body can only take so much and the rickshaw puller is running himself into an early grave, but it's the only job he knows and he would sooner run through the hottest day imaginable than beg on the streets. Rickshaw pullers evidently have their own little community, with great comradeship existing between them, and they take immense pride in what they do. To them, begging on the streets is total humiliation, the last resort. In the monsoon season, when torrential rain means Calcutta is under a foot of water, their services are required even more because the city's office workers mustn't get their feet wet. Human horses are running all over Indian cities in their thousands and they will do so until they drop.

As I leaned on a handrail near those traffic lights studying the chaos of Calcutta's road traffic, I noticed a young Indian girl of about 15 right in the centre of this very busy road. She was holding a baby and standing about 200 yards from where the vehicles pulled up at the lights. This is quite a common sight in India. When the lights turn red and the vehicles stop, these desperate young women and girls dash over to the cars, pleading passionately to the drivers and passengers for money. This girl, however, was standing right in the middle of the road, with traffic literally brushing either side of her. I looked on in amazement at what was happening. This girl was pleading quite hysterically for the vehicles to stop before they reached the traffic lights, her voice only just audible above the din. She was pleading with her life. What she was doing was extremely dangerous. I feared for her safety. Vehicles seemed to be coming at her from all directions. For a second it looked as though she was trying to kill both herself and her baby. But she was begging for help and for money. She must have been at the end of her tether. Surely, I thought, she must get knocked over. It was a horrible spectacle. Needless to say, not one vehicle stopped. She kept holding her baby up to the oncoming traffic. She was just one among millions of beggars all over India. Then she noticed me watching her. To her I was white and therefore affluent. She dashed through the maze of traffic to get to me.

"Please, please. Baby, baby," she kept pleading, trying to tell me of course that she was begging for her baby. I gave her a few rupees and the gratitude in her face seemed to say that I'd saved both her life and the child's. She then followed me all the way back to the hotel. "Please, please. Baby, baby - more," she kept saying. Obviously she couldn't speak English too well. I had a good long look at this girl by my side. Both she and the baby were dressed in rags. She looked terribly thin and I wondered what a desperate existence she must lead. She wouldn't be able to get a job and the father of her child probably didn't want to know her. There was desperation in all her actions. I couldn't help but feel sympathy for her. She was like thousands of girls throughout India who spend their lives begging in the streets. Yet this girl did have one thing going for her. She had a beauty all her own. Some of these Indian girls, even in the rags they wear, are strikingly beautiful and I was struck by the thought that this girl, because of her looks, could be drawn into prostitution. Whatever we think of prostitution, and some people do have strong moral views about it, one thing is for sure and that is that it will always be a part of this world we live in. However offensive it may be to some, it's here to stay. It's not known as the world's oldest profession for nothing. Calcutta, like a lot of other Indian cities' is rife with it and the destitute poor of any Third Word country are easily drawn into it by their desperate circumstances. That girl, begging amid that mass of traffic and regularly risking life and limb, could be one such person. Think of that young girl arriving home - did I say home? She might of course not even have had a roof over her head - she would have experienced a day of sheer horror and abuse from drivers in the streets. She would have been kicked and spat at and she would be in a state of despair, depression and despondency at her position. Her emaciated baby would be crying continuously through lack of food, but, after a bad day on the streets, its mother would be unable to feed it. She is destitute, totally impoverished and the only thing she owns is the rags she and the baby are wearing. She is alone in the world and extremely frightened. She contemplates killing herself and there are very probably two choices left to her - death or prostitution. Does she have the courage to kill herself and the baby? No, she can't. The survival instinct is strong. Surely someone will help me, she thinks every day on waking up and dragging herself through the nightmare of begging on the street. Then, probably at the lowest moment in her young life, and certainly the most vulnerable, she is approached by a pimp, a man who controls prostitutes. He promises her easy money.

"How can you let your baby starve?" he asks. Having been approached many times by these people, the girl knows what's next. This man wants her body, not necessarily for himself, but for others. "Make some real money and feed your baby," he tells her. She is being asked to engage in sexual intercourse for money, to involve herself in another form of begging - pleading with passers-by in Calcutta's streets to take her body. She has resisted this path repeatedly, though she is sorely tempted as her baby cries for food. She knows she will hate what she will be asked to do, but her baby is dying and she has to convince herself there is no other course of action.

After seeing life at possibly its lowest level out on those Indian streets I couldn't condemn the evils of prostitution outright, however unseemly, repulsive or unpleasant some people might think it is. I know it goes against all

Christian beliefs, but who am I to judge? How does one survive in such a world? That young girl surely has as much right to feed her baby as young mothers in the West. If anyone reading this book could understand the hell of being poor in India, they might then grasp that this girl is at death's door. I have three grandchildren. The oldest are six and three. If they had been born in Calcutta's slums, they could be scavenging on rubbish tips for food. This particular part of my book is probably the most difficult for me to write because I am trying to communicate the sheer misery of this existence and the fact that for some it is like hell on earth. Think about what I'm trying to describe, then imagine something 10 times worse. If that pretty Indian girl does give in to grisly temptation it is because she has no other choice. If I am to condemn anyone, it has to be the pimps who sweet-talk the girls into this degrading work because once a girl turns to prostitution her life could well be worse than before. These bully-boy pimps specialise in dishing out regular beatings to the girls under their control. The one consolation for the girl would be that she would be able to feed her baby and herself from her miserly earnings. All hope of large sums of money would be abandoned at an early stage and the girl would live in extreme fear of her pimp. I bracket these people with paedophiles and drug traffickers. They really are destroying lives.

Thousands of girls, some as young as 10 and under, are prostitutes in India. Some are even kidnapped and sold into this evil trade and transported to work in brothels hundreds of miles away. They are held against their will and forced to have their bodies abused. If they manage to escape and are unlucky enough to be caught they can expect to be beaten and even killed. Some girls may find suicide is the only escape from such immoral work. Often only the hardened survive. A lot of these girls are country girls. Some are even sold by their parents. Aids is definitely on the increase in India and hundreds, maybe thousands, of these girls risk contracting it. When they are dying and unable to ply their sordid trade any more, their pimps may allow them back to their villages because they are of no further use. But once back in their home village, instead of finishing their days with love and sympathy, which they undoubtedly deserve, they are shunned and treated like lepers. Because of what they have become, they bring great shame on their families. They are ostracised by all in the village and if it is discovered that they have Aids they will literally be driven away and banished forever. They may well have to return to the town or city where they did their unsavoury work. They would certainly get no compassion from their former pimps - more likely, perhaps, would be a terrible beating from which they will probably never recover. That beating might hasten death, which could be a blessing, as the girls would be sure to die of Aids in a gutter somewhere. They could well be dead by the time they are 20. I do not exaggerate when I say that thousands of young girls are experiencing that life in India today.

That young girl I saw on the streets could one day find herself working in a brothel and as I write I'm reminded of what the two assistant managers had told me one evening at the Kenilworth Hotel. I was talking to them in their office and the topic of conversation turned to Calcutta's nightlife. I was told there were at least 200,000 prostitutes in the city. These staggering, startling figures take some believing, but that's what I was told. Even more disturbing was the massive increase in child prostitution that I was told about. Again my thoughts turn to the girl I met in that busy street. I'm convinced that, human nature being what it is, she will in the end do anything to survive. She simply has to feed her baby. What a choice for one so young to have to make. Unfortunately, the alternatives are not abundant.

Do not think for a moment that I am advocating the

legislation of prostitution, because I'm not. With the strong Christian faith that I now have I couldn't possibly go along with that, wherever it may be. But this is India that I'm talking about and that young girl is very much part of today's India - and if she were to turn to prostitution, I for one could not criticise her. She is under enormous pressure to provide for her baby and ensure its survival as well as her own. That girl is fighting for her life. It is not unlike a person who is dying from starvation. The intense hunger generated by not eating properly for days or even a week must be too awful to contemplate. One would finish up just eating anything to survive. Rats have been mentioned in this book before - well, when you are fighting to live even they become viable as food. Survival instinct is powerful. Survivors of concentration camps, where horrific conditions prevailed, testify to this. Some years ago, survivors of a plane crash in South America's Andes infamously ate the flesh of their dead fellow passengers to survive because the food had run out while they were marooned high in the mountains awaiting rescue. The body's need for food is paramount and hunger can drive a person mad, so how on earth could I criticise that girl? No way could I condemn her for selling her body if that is what she decided to do. How would any of us react in similar circumstances? I could weep for her. Hopefully, like those plane crash survivors, she will survive one way or another.

Walking back to the hotel, the girl never left my side. If she said please once, she must have said it 100 times. One would have had to have been a hard so-and-so to have ignored her pleas, which were intermingled with crying and whimpering. At the hotel gates I stood with her for about 10 minutes. I'm sure the passers-by, the beggars in the streets and the hotel guests must have wondered what was going on. In a strange way, I didn't want to leave her, but I had to because I had to get ready for my evening flight home.

After about an hour inside the hotel I ventured out once more to the front gates. She was still there with her baby. She pleaded so emotionally for the child and herself. I stood with her, more out of pity than anything else. I tried to comfort her and I must admit I had the deepest sympathy it is possible to have for another human being. She looked so ill and just the spectacle of her was enough to leave me quite perturbed. She and her baby really were a pitiful sight I'm sure she would have hung on to me if she could. Because I had showed kindness to her I was her friend and there can't be many friends for a young girl fending for herself on Calcutta's street. It outrages me to think she could easily fall under the control of some cowardly pimp. She could be continually knocked about. On reflection I only wish I'd had the courage to take her and her baby into the Kenilworth Hotel and give her a meal she could otherwise only dream about. It would have been interesting to see what the hotel management would have done about it. Would they have allowed this low-caste Indian girl into the hotel because she was with me? Would they have allowed her, dressed in rags as she was, to pass through those impressive glass doors? Because behind those doors there lay, for her, a different world. As well as I'd got on with those two assistant managers, they would simply have been doing their job if they had refused her entry, which, incidentally, I think they would have done. Nevertheless, I would have loved to have put it to the test. I'm sure the bell captain would have messed himself on seeing that young girl and her baby walking into that hotel. I should have challenged the caste system by insisting that the girl was with me. Just imagine - for two glorious hours I could have made her feel like a princess.

"Goodbye, Mr Brian, do come again, won't you," said the assistant manager as I shook his hand. I'd said goodbye to other members of staff at the hotel and I was on my way home. I was lucky enough once more to have the services of Balaram as the taxi pulled out of the hotel car park and into the city streets. I peered through the windows to see if the girl was still there, but she had disappeared, vanished from my life forever. I didn't even know her name. I was returning to my comfortable life in England and leaving her to those streets filled with leprosy, tuberculosis, cholera, malaria, polio and sexually transmitted diseases, as well as countless other illnesses. I can only hope and pray that in whatever she does or whatever she is to become she finds some measure of hope, peace and contentment in her life. I doubt it, though, because her future can only be bleak. Perhaps she does not even have one.

Travelling through those city streets was also one final unforgettable experience. Seeing the misery on those streets and amid the bustees, some on the roadside, filled me with despair once more. Through the taxi window I could see the pavements packed as usual with beggars and pavement-dwellers, who compete for space with small stalls selling cauliflowers, potatoes, apples, oranges, bananas and indeed most fruits and vegetables. The stall holders must make some kind of living, because there are thousands of them all over the city.

Calcutta is a city that I do have a certain affection for, but no way could I have said that when I'd landed at Dum Dum Airport two weeks earlier. To see Calcutta in torrents of rain is an unforgettably grim experience, but with the sun out it's different. The daily misery is still there, of course, but what stands out is the friendliness of Calcutta's inhabitants. Just about all the people I spoke to were extremely friendly, but it's that kind of city. I now feel lucky to have seen Calcutta again and on that final day I had an odd feeling of sadness that I was seeing the sheer squalor and deprivation of that most run-down of all cities in the old

British Empire for the last time. At the airport it was goodbye to my friend Balaram, who had really gone out of his way to take me around the city of his birth. He seemed to know every inch of it.

"Goodbye, Mr Brian," he said as he warmly shook hands. Then he was gone and lost amid a crowd of beggars. My flight was due at 9.50pm and I settled down for a good two hours' wait. I was getting the usual butterflies in my stomach. I wonder how other passengers feel as they're waiting in airport lounges, because I'm far from relaxed. I fidget nervously at the prospect of what lies ahead. Although leaving this world holds no fears for me, it's the very moment of death, the fatal impact, that scares me. The thought of some horrendous plane crash has always frightened the wits out of me, although I have to say that if I were to die in an air crash I probably wouldn't know a thing about it. It's strange what sort of consolation one can draw while waiting to board an aircraft, mine being that if the plane I was destined to travel on was about to crash I would at least have the comfort of knowing it was British-built. It's not that Indian Airways have a bad safety record, because they don't, but if I was to die in a foreign aircraft and as I sat in the lounge that evening, my consolation was that I would at least be flying British Airways.

Looking out of the small plane windows a little later I could see fireworks being let off, seemingly all over Calcutta. It was to celebrate some Hindu festival, and as the lights and flashes beneath me receded as the aircraft reached for the sky I was able to look back on another fantastic two weeks in India. Let me say that if you lead a relatively uneventful life and are looking for some excitement, India is the place to visit. It seems so different from any other countries I have visited. But, if you can't stand seeing the most unbelievable poverty there is, two words of advice - stay away. I knew as I sat on that plane that the memories of those two weeks just wouldn't leave me. How could some of the most memorable moments I have ever experienced in my life ever be allowed to desert me? Looking back on that fortnight, I feel exactly as I did following my first three weeks in India, namely that I had got more from such a short period than from many a year of my life. How fortunate I have been to visit India again. Surely, if I was ever to visit it again it couldn't be as good for a third time, and, as I sat on that plane, I knew my place was with my wife and family and I couldn't wait to get home to lovely Market Deeping.

On the plane I still couldn't sleep. I expected to be fast asleep by the time we touched down in New Delhi, which was about an hour after leaving Calcutta. But I think I was so over-tired that I couldn't concentrate on sleeping. In view of all that had happened during my stay in India it was little wonder I couldn't sleep.

"This is the captain speaking. Due to thick fog over Heathrow Airport we are unable to land, so we will touch down in Manchester until the fog clears," came the voice from the cockpit as we neared London. True to form it had happened again. I couldn't believe I could be booked on four flights to India and back and have problems with all of them. I knew it wasn't too much to be alarmed about, but four consecutive flights with some mess-up or other takes some beating. Evidently these things do happen. The other passengers and myself sat in the plane on the tarmac at Manchester for three hours as we waited for the morning fog to lift at Heathrow. Finally, we took off and just 35 minutes later the plane was landing at Heathrow. There, I was met by my neighbour, who, incidentally, struggled with my suitcase. On arriving home his wife told me how ill I looked. She was absolutely right. I was suffering from extreme exhaustion and I'd lost weight. My trip to India had taken an awful lot out of me.

As I sat at home that day with my family I just couldn't believe that just hours earlier I'd been walking the streets of Calcutta. My mind was in turmoil over all that had happened and all that I'd seen. I felt like I'd woken up from a dream. But it wasn't a dream. What I saw was for real, and as my three grandkids jumped and rolled over me on the kitchen floor I couldn't help but feel the presence of India so close to me that I could almost reach out and touch it. And yet it also seemed a million miles away, though among what seemed like a thousand memories of India, there were two that just wouldn't leave me. One was that oh-so-dramatic and emotional farewell scene at Ranchi railway station. Goodbyes can be so sad and I can visualise so clearly in my mind the whole atmosphere of that evening. I can still see Albina and the sisters waving furiously as the train pulled out of the station amid the smoke, steam and noise. I shall carry those final moments to my grave. Even the sisters, writing to me since my return home, have described that incident as upsetting and heartbreaking. One other memory also won't leave me - that young Indian girl begging on Calcutta's streets just hours before I flew out of the city. Tears streaming down her face, she was pleading pathetically for money to feed her baby and herself. To me, she symbolised what being poor in India was and I know she was certainly not receiving the love I was experiencing on my arrival home. It will be a long time before that girl is erased from my memory. I had a lot to be thankful for. I had returned home safely to my wife and family and I also know there's no place like home. I had again been to the back of beyond in deepest Bihar in north east India and perhaps one has to leave one's comfortable English home every so often to visit a Third World country, because believe me it puts one's whole life into perspective. England, my England, the Union Jack and all that. Honestly, there's no place like it.

Chapter Twelve

The Golden Vision

The horrendous plane crash did happen. Just over 18 hours after I left India, where the lights were still flickering from the great Hindu festival, two jet airliners collided in mid-air in the skies above New Delhi International Airport - those very same skies from which my British Airways jet had descended for its stopover from Calcutta to pick up passengers. The head-on collision was the world's worst. It was 6.30pm on a Tuesday evening when a Saudi Arabian Boeing 747 took off from New Delhi with 312 people on board, bound for Dhahran. At the same time, a Kazakhstani airliner from Chimkent carrying 27 passengers and crew was beginning its descent to the same airport. The smaller, Russian-built, aircraft was sharing a flight corridor with the Saudi jet. The airport control tower had told the Russian pilot of the departing Saudi plane that although both aircraft were in the same two-way lane, they were satisfied nevertheless that the measuring altitude was well within the safety margin, with one plane flying well above the other. But New Delhi's tracking system is evidently 25 years behind the times. No blame has therefore been attached to the air traffic controllers. India has a terribly outdated air traffic control system and because of that 339 people perished. There were no survivors from that collision.

The Saudi aircraft was travelling at 500 km/h when it hit the Russian-made plane, causing both to explode on impact. A great ball of fire lit up the sky. The crash sent the Saudi plane to the ground with such speed that it made a three-metre-deep hole. The Kazakh plane plunged inexorably downwards, despite the frantic efforts of its pilot to regain control. The collision had caused fuel tanks to explode and people, luggage and seats spiralled to the ground. After some hours, fire engines made their way through the little country lanes to the two crash sites. The smouldering wreckage of the Saudi aircraft contained graphic details of the sheer horror that its passengers must have experienced. A young farm worker, one of the first to arrive at the scene of this most horrific of all mid-air collisions, said there were burnt bodies everywhere. Body parts could even be seen hanging in the kikar trees. Everywhere he walked through the tangled and burning wreckage he found charred corpses. He and other local people fought through smoke, flames and excessive heat, and had handkerchiefs covering their faces to keep out the stench of burning flesh. What those passengers must have experienced is almost too much to contemplate. The relatives of those on board, having said goodbye to their loved ones at the airport less than an hour earlier, rushed to the crash scene. It was nearly impossible to identify most of the bodies, so badly were they burned and disfigured. Often it was a remaining trace of a piece of clothing that offered up the vital clue. One man, after many hours of searching for his son, finally accepted his death when he found a severed hand with a familiar wrist watch still attached.

India's civil aviation authorities immediately launched an inquiry into the double air disaster. New Delhi International Airport is one of the busiest in the world. Its air traffic increases by 10 per cent each year. A former executive director of the International Passenger Airlines Association has said: "India has a wretchedly outmoded air traffic control and flight surveillance system. The hazards are enormous." I've mentioned previously in this book that India has a good record on plane crashes, and I believe that still applies. With a traffic system so out of date as this, though, the door remains open for more terrible disasters like the one I have described. I've read recently that India's tracking system is to be upgraded. If that is so, then what a pity it took the loss of 339 lives for something to be done. I know from first-hand experience that enormous problems are generated by the unreliability of flights in India, and I can vouch for the fact that it hardly breeds confidence among passengers. When the Ursuline sisters at Tongo first heard of this collision they feared that I might have been among the dead. As they didn't have the full details, I'm told, many prayers were being said for me. Sister Bernadette at Gotra told me later in a letter that when she heard about the crash she lit a candle every hour until she heard that it wasn't a British plane and that I was safe. This, of course, was the sister who had said on that very last morning as we came out of the chapel at the Ranchi convent school: "Have no fear. You will get home safely." She was proved right, of course, and sitting at home after my return I heard the dreadful news on TV that all those people had perished in the skies that I'd been in only hours before.

Goodbye, England's rose. The extraordinary, irreplaceable and irresistible Diana was dead. Never in my life have I known such an outpouring of shared grief as that which greeted the unbelievable news that she had been killed in a car crash in Paris in the early hours of August 31, 1997. Like Mother Teresa, she gave great love and compassion to the poor and underprivileged. Most importantly, she cut across racial barriers and that's why, I believe, the princess was loved by so many coloured people. One particular photo taken of her in Pakistan not long before her death shows such humanity as she cradles a dying child. Who can forget her work for the victims of civil war in Bosnia, where children had their legs blown off by land mines. The images of her shaking hands with Aids sufferers and cuddling babies with leprosy also live long in the memory. When I first met Mother Teresa at her Missionaries of Charity home on November 4, 1991, she was quite thrilled at the prospect of meeting the princess. When I had my audience with her, the forthcoming visit was among the things we discussed. She was due to meet Diana in Calcutta in February 1992, during the princess's tour of India. But, only weeks after I met her, Mother Teresa had a heart attack while in Mexico. She was rushed to a hospital in America before being transferred to Rome, where she recuperated. So when the princess visited the Mother House in Calcutta, Mother Teresa was not there to meet her. Not to be defeated, Diana flew to Rome, and, at the bedside of this great Christian, a most unlikely friendship developed. A deep bond was sealed. "Diana has a beautiful spirit," said Mother Teresa after that first meeting. How ironic it was therefore, that these two women, who had given such beautiful love (that's the only way I can describe it) to millions of people, should die within five days of each other. Two women, two dynamic forces who were drawn together by their wonderful capacity for giving love, are now united in death. Two women from the most differing backgrounds and with an age difference of 51 years had become more than just firm friends, and one might well ask what they had in common. One was born at the turn of the century in one of the poorest countries in the world and would go on to become its best-known nun for her work with the poorest of the poor, dying of a heart attack at the age of 87. The other was an aristocrat's daughter born into one of the wealthy families of England, who would marry her prince and become the most beautiful and talked-about princess there's ever been. She would die in the most tragic circumstances at the age of just 36, devastating a whole nation. Both will go down in history as two of the greatest personalities of their age. One simple word, though, binds these two very different women: Love. That's what they had in common - the capacity to give love to one's fellow human beings with a warmth and humanity that would touch so many lives. Yet, though they had this special gift of loving, they both had their critics. Both have suffered severe an unwarranted criticism, as well as inevitable bad publicity. It's as though any person doing good work in this world must be ridiculed unmercifully. These two certainly were.

Mother Teresa was always her own woman and if something needed to be said, she said it. She could be quite controversial. She would often answer her critics simply by saying that she was doing God's work. "I work for him," was her explanation. She was strongly opposed to any kind of birth control, even though she lived in a city of squalor and poverty where she had seen thousands of babies dying through malnutrition. She was passionate in her beliefs, describing abortion as a form of murder. Among the accusations levelled at her was that she exploited the poor to promote the Catholic church. Her outspokenness was legendary. Many years ago, a Westerner walking the streets of Calcutta came across an abandoned baby. It was clearly sick and had been left to die or be taken care of by some kind person. This Westerner was such a person and, having heard of Mother Teresa's orphanage, he took the undernourished child there. Now, Mother Teresa had never turned anyone away and she took the baby from this man, but to his astonishment she told him the child was really his responsibility and that this had been God's way of informing him that the baby was his.

Being so outspoken left a certain British Prime Minister lost for words. I love the story of when this frail, seemingly inoffensive little old lady met the indomitable Margaret Thatcher. After getting off the plane that had brought her to Heathrow Airport, Mother Teresa travelled through the streets of London to Downing Street. She was most shocked to see how some of the city's poor lived on the streets, and, on meeting Mrs Thatcher, she must have infuriated Maggie when she said she would pray for those poor people. Just to ruffle Mrs Thatcher's feathers further, Mother Teresa told her she should tackle the problem further by clearing all the dispossessed from London's streets. Mrs Thatcher must have looked at her guest in disbelief, as if to say "nobody speaks to me like that, not even you." Behind that frozen look, which many a nervous cabinet minister must have experienced before she sacked him, the Prime Minister must have been thinking "you go back to India and look after your poor, because I'm more than capable of looking after mine, thank you very much". The story goes that the Iron Lady was humbled. She had underestimated the Angel of Calcutta.

There was a quite scandalous TV programme about Mother Teresa on Channel 4 in November, 1994. This documentary was so biased against her that it made one wonder if this was the same Mother Teresa who had given such Christian love to the world. Cardinal Hulme, Archbishop of Westminster, rightly accused Channel 4 of screening a grotesque caricature of her. The programme criticised her from start to finish, accusing her of mixing with sinners such as dubious political figures and failed dictators and accepting money from them for her charities. My answer to that is to ask: Did Jesus Christ not mix with sinners? It was a dirty, muck-raking programme. What was so annoying was that the good she had done in the world was hardly mentioned and not one person who admired her work was interviewed. What fairness is there in a programme like that? On hearing of this criticism, Mother Teresa said she would pray for the programme makers.

When I heard of her death, I was, quite surprisingly, not too upset. That second time I'd met her, in November 1996, I really didn't think she could live much longer, so ill did she look. She did, in fact, live another 11 months, and I didn't like the thought of her suffering, so to me her death came as a certain kind of relief. Even her funeral was not without controversy. It was said Mother Teresa would not have liked the state funeral the Indian government gave her. Dignitaries flew in from all over the world and, of course, had grandstand views of the service and the procession, leaving the poor of Calcutta, who she had served for over 50 years, unable to see the cortege because of the vast crowds.

My lasting memory of this great Christian was that she was surprisingly ordinary and had this gift of making everyone she met feel important. I found it so incredibly easy to strike up conversation with her and because of this I felt I'd known her for years. She evidently looked on Diana, Princess of Wales as a surrogate daughter and I for one will always think of them as being inextricably drawn together. The people's princess and Mother Teresa gave a wonderful combination of love to the world, and in Diana's life it was so tragically cut short. As I write, the country still mourns her death.

As I come to the end of my second book on India, what are my thoughts as the country moves forward to the year 2000? I suppose my thoughts will always be for its people, and because of them I will always think of the caste system and its unfairness. I just wish someone would explain to me the difference between apartheid, which was practised in South Africa until it was formally abolished six years ago, and the caste system of India, because I believe there is no difference at all. In both cases, it's segregation and discrimination on a massive scale. The caste system is hardly fair because the majority of the people governed by it are downtrodden. It seems to be a segregation policy for the four main castes - to be born in one of the lower castes, or, worse, an untouchable, is to remain trapped for life. The rich Hindus of the high castes completely control 80 per cent of the lower castes, and very unpleasantly, too, I might add. This, then, is discrimination. South Africa's official government policy during the period of apartheid was one of racial segregation. In other words, the tiny white minority controlled the black and coloured people, who had very little to say in the running of the country. This also happens in India, with segregation and discrimination both blatant. So what's the difference between South Africa's apartheid system of old and the caste system of India, which still enures. The only difference is that in South Africa it was white against black and in India it's black against black. The world was forever criticising South Africa's oppressive apartheid rules, but very rarely have I heard India's caste system criticised in the same way. England didn't play South Africa at cricket - or indeed any other sport - for 30 years because of apartheid and we were told that would not change until the system did. Yet, my whole point is that India, which discriminates against the majority of its wretchedly poor people, has never been criticised in the same way. Never has there been any talk of not playing India at sport. India's treatment of its poor is shocking. Go and see those shacks in the City of Joy and you will quickly discover the harsh reality of the caste system. That system is just as bad as apartheid. Years ago, when I was in the Army, I spent a whole day in Cape Town, South Africa. That day I saw how the poor people lived as a result of apartheid. They lived in their thousands in despicable little huts and in poverty on a scale I've never been able to forget. Let me say, though, that the slums I've seen in India are equally as bad as what I witnessed in Cape Town that day. A slum is a slum wherever it may be and after seeing the slums of both those countries, I fail to see a difference between them.

There's a factory in Calcutta which employs hundreds of children, who work 10 to 12 hours a day in absolutely terrible conditions. It's a throwback to the world of Oliver Twist, of an England long since consigned to the past, an England of slave labour. India is notorious for its child labour. It is plainly exploitation of children on a massive scale and here again the caste system has a lot to answer for, as it is the children of the poor who work for as little as 25p per day. In many a backstreet or dingy lane in any big city in India there is a drab, dishevelled sweatshop where 10-year-old kids spend their lives. Untold numbers of children work this way throughout India and though no one seems to know for sure exactly how many, it could run to millions. In these sweatshops, children slave away their lives, the heat, stench, smoke, dust and general filth leaving them looking shockingly ill and withdrawn, with signs of gross malnutrition. If they happened to be employed in the textile industry, these children would be tethered to sewing machines, living a monotonous life that could send them out of their tiny minds. They are employed by entrepreneurs, the fat cats of India who exploit the poor with seeming disregard for the tender years of those from whose toil they make their fortunes. Although very young, these children could be tied to these jobs for years because they are their family's breadwinner. The child might well be supporting a mother plus brothers and sisters because their father has died. One of the disturbing aspects of this child labour is that a lot of the clothes made by it finishes up in the big stores of the Western world. Children are working all over India in slave labour conditions, in firework factories, in brickworks and, in some states, even on road repair teams. They wouldn't know anything about going to school. What dignity have these poor little kids got as they work away in these factories? I've read recently that footballs made in India are now being used for major football matches in England. They are being made by child labour for an absolute pittance and some of the children making them might be working as long as 15 hours a day. So when the richest and most famous of all football clubs in Britain, Manchester United, whose wealth is boosted by an incomparable merchandising empire, kicks off its next match, spare a thought for how and where that football may have been made. There's a good chance it has been handmade and stitched by little Indian children with terribly sore, bloody hands and fingers, who are the extremely cheap labour behind too much of India's economy.

Those who have read this book will surely by now have realised that I am proud to be British. For all its faults, I happen to believe Britain is by far the finest country in the world. Britons are probably at their worst when running the old country down. We can be critical of whatever government is in power at any given time, and I am not averse to making my views known from time to time. But what I am proud of is Britain's colonial past. At one time the empire extended to all corners of the globe. One has only to look at a map of the world from 60 years ago to see the countries that Britain was helping towards independence. I think my pride stems from my National Service days in the Army over 44 years ago, when I was in Hong Kong. Only a few months ago, Britain finally handed Hong Kong over to the Chinese. It had been a success story for Britain. Not all our former colonies have prospered like Hong Kong. It was a triumphant achievement. The economy is booming and people there lead generally successful lives. I remember my Army days there well and watching the closing ceremonies of Britain's rule on TV, with Governor Chris Patten sailing away in the Royal Yacht Britannia and brass bands playing 'Rule Britannia' and 'Land of Hope and Glory', brought tears to my eyes. How emotional it all was. Hong Kong is steeped in British history and the 99-year lease was up. My one big hope for Hong Kong now is that the Chinese continue to let it go on being a success story and try not to change it.

The old British Empire is never better illustrated than in India. Critics of Britain's colonial past would probably say that the British grew rich from India and that the country was ruled by a gang of robbers who just wanted to fleece it. There may, of course, have been some truth in this, but it's a fact that for the majority of the time the British spent in India, they governed it as well as they did their own country. That meant India had the best administrators there were. Recently the country celebrated the 50th anniversary of independence from Britain and they have been quite successful years, but India today lives on a time bomb and there is the feeling that anything might happen. It really is a violent country and since independence it has had more than just skirmishes with its neighbour Pakistan - there have been two all-out wars. The state of Kashmir seems to be the most potent source of conflict between the two countries. India insists on holding on to its northern territory, much to the annoyance of Pakistan. India being predominantly Hindu and Pakistan being Muslim is of course the fundamental reason for the continued hostility between the two countries.

During the years of imperial rule, many thousands of British soldiers and Indian people were killed. Mistakes obviously were made and when the Hindus and Muslims started fighting each other, thousands were slaughtered, with the British soldiers acting as policemen and pleasing no one. After 150 years, when their presence became intolerable and all Indians wanted the British out of their country, Mahatma Gandhi began to lead the way to independence and is not forgotten to this day. Gandhi was murdered just before independence, and what a figure he is in Indian history. He was so revered by most Indians, but obviously he had his enemies. He actually went on a hunger strike, saying he wouldn't eat again until the Hindus and Muslims stopped fighting each other. He was virtually at death's door when the fighting stopped. Thousands had been killed. Partition saw the forming of the new state of Pakistan and all India's Muslims migrated there en bloc. So, after 150 years, India had its independence. It makes one wonder how India would have managed without the British influence. It could have been ruled by despots or some corrupt Marxist regime, or heaven knows what. So I refuse to believe that the Raj did a bad job in India.

The very sound of the word vision conjures up what to me is one of the definitions of the word. It is a person or thing of extraordinary beauty. I must confess I have never personally seen a vision nor a religious experience connected to some supernatural event while in the subcontinent, or anywhere else, for that matter. One might think that, living at an Indian convent school for a week with Catholic Ursuline sisters, this might well have been a possibility because nuns, of course, do spend a considerable amount of time in prayers. One vision I have seen in reality, though, is "The Golden Vision". This is the subtitle of this book and the name I have given to this final chapter. It is also the name I give for what I believe might be possible when I think about the future of the Ursuline convent school at Tongo, so please allow me for just a few moments to describe "The Golden Vision".

I first set eyes on "The Golden Vision" in 1962 and it was a sight never to be forgotten, for what I saw was a blond ghost of an athlete who may well have arrived from Olympus. He was a cultured pearl of a soccer player who played for Everton (Everton won the league championship in the 1962/63 season and were the finest team in the country) and was idolised at Goodison Park, Liverpool. In the early 60s I lived in that part of England and watched him regularly. He had the angelic looks of a choirboy and with his blond hair and his small, frail-looking physique he led the attack with such smoothness and style, gliding in a ghost-like manner past defenders as if he was skating on ice. He became a legend and his name was Alex Young - and he was called "The Golden Vision", this name also being given to a TV documentary about him. With the ball at his feet, Alex Young was a person of extraordinary beauty. His exquisite and refined skills convinced me that his play was more accustomed to another planet. Surprisingly, he was not all that well-known outside of Liverpool. The same would never be true of such a player today because he would be worth millions of pounds, although it must be said that his dazzling skills were not always appreciated. He played just seven times for Scotland, a complete travesty for such a genius of a footballer. The adulation he received at Goodison still lives in my memory. Surely no soccer player could have been hero-worshipped more by his own fans. I can still visualise the thousands in the stands leaping out of their seats whenever he had the ball. These were the days when 70,000 people would be at the ground. I've only ever seen one other player bring the crowd to its feet in the same way and that was George Best. High praise indeed. If I could turn the clock back to those far-off days, loving walking as I do, I would willingly walk from my home to Liverpool for just 90 minutes of seeing his artistic and ghostly play. Needless to say, after my home town club, Peterborough United (Posh), Everton's results are always the next I look for. Yes, I've seen "The Golden Vision". He became my all-time favourite player. Evertonians will tell you there's never been anyone like him before or since.

Please do not think I can see any comparison between this unique soccer player and that school at Tongo because I can't. But "The Golden Vision" is a name I've borrowed to describe the school. A vision, as I've explained, is something beautiful and it so happens that the very name of "The Golden Vision" describes perfectly for me my ambitions for the school. That Tongo school can become a place of extraordinary beauty. Just like Alex Young, that school is special and it definitely has a hold on my heart. My own vision, and also my ambition, therefore, is to make that school one of the finest in southern Bihar. I do realise that it may be just a pipe dream, but we all have dreams, don't we, and this is mine. I also realise that the finest schools in India would, without question, be the big private schools, where the rich Hindus would send their children, and the Tongo school could never compete with that. But what I do know is that an ordinary girls' school right in the very heart of the Indian countryside has enormous potential to become, with development, a very fine school indeed.

One thing is preventing the Tongo school from realising that potential - money. Without it, the school could deteriorate very rapidly into something very shabby indeed. In places it is falling apart and much repair work is required. Money is needed in order to make a start. The school wall has now been rebuilt, and with strong iron gates in place, security is probably as good as it's ever been. As I've already explained, six new classrooms have also been built and are fully operational, giving even more Indian children the chance to be educated. The school is nevertheless still in decline and decay and money is needed to bring it back to its former glory. On my first visit to Tongo I was reasonably impressed by what I'd seen, but, five years on, I'd seen a marked change, and unless the Indian government is prepared to help with those much-needed repairs, the school will deteriorate even further. Painting all the buildings would be a good start. My ambition is to continue to see the school progress and become what I know it could become.

With more classrooms hopefully on the way, the school's future doesn't look that bad, and the fact that the only other school in the village is for boys means there's no "competition". As I travelled through Bihar down those little country lanes, every so often I would come across a little one-roomed mud hut stuck in a field somewhere. Perhaps 80 children would be in attendance. These little brick or mud huts seemed to be scattered everywhere. Of course, they are grossly overcrowded. Indian children are desperate for education. Their keenness is overwhelming. They will willingly walk 10 miles to school every day, often to find that the teacher hasn't turned up. So, although there are many of these one-hut schools, none of them seems to be working properly.

The Indian constitution guarantees an education to all children up to the age of 14, but it is a fact that out of India's massive population less than 50 per cent of its children are being educated. Also, as I've already mentioned in this book, many children in the countryside are needed to help their parents in the fields, so they will remain illiterate. The only hope, as I see it, is the expansion of the bigger schools, like the one at Tongo. The convent schools I've visited in Bihar, all run by the Ursuline sisters, are extremely good in comparison to the one-hut schools. This is where I feel the future lies for India's education of its rural population. The development of Tongo school could do wonders for that area of Bihar, as even more children would be able to walk chirpily to school. That is my ambition for the school at Tongo, my "Golden Vision".

It has taken just over 12 months to write this second book about India. How Jeffrey Archer writes a novel in just over two weeks defeats me. I'd actually hoped that with retirement, I'd finish this second book much sooner. With more time on my hands than when I wrote *My Indian Journey*, I really did think I could complete it quicker. I've since wondered how on earth I managed to write that book while still working. Perhaps the reason this book has taken longer is that I was looking for some sort of perfection. I now realise that perfection can never be achieved. I've settled for what I know best, which is being myself. The real aim for any writer is to maintain the reader's interest. No book will ever sell if it doesn't do that. Only time will tell if I've succeeded or failed miserably. People locally have been asking about my new book. Some have even placed orders for it. But nothing is guaranteed in this world and I've had really hard periods during the writing of this book, when I've struggled to keep the momentum going. Generally, though, I've enjoyed writing it. Many a time the humour I found in India was what kept me going. It acted as a lift. I've thought of Dr Kar in that slum in Calcutta known as The City of Joy, and how he was splitting his sides with laughter when telling me I wasn't very bright. Maybe when he reads this book - and I will certainly send him one - he might actually compliment me by saying he enjoyed it. Above all, I hope he laughs while reading it. He really is one of the humanitarians of India and if I can bring a smile to his face amid the quite unbelievable squalor of that slum, I will really feel that I've achieved something.

As I come to the end of this book, my memories of India are enormous. Of course, if I'd never sponsored Albina Kujur I'm absolutely sure I'd never have dreamt of going there. Although the country held a certain fascination for me years ago in my school days, I never thought I'd visit it. Now I have been twice. Seeing that squalor in Calcutta, how the other half lives, really was an education. I will never forget what I saw that day in the slums of the City of Joy. It made me realise more than ever how incredibly lucky I've been in my life. How would I have survived in that slum if I'd been born in India? I'm reminded of the American-born multi-billionaire John Paul Getty I, without question one of the richest men in the world when he was alive. This legendary oil magnate had one great fear in his life, namely that when he died he would return through reincarnation as one of the street kids of Calcutta. He believed that on death the soul transmigrates or is born again into another body. Well John Paul Getty, if you are out there as one of those street kids, may God help you because those kids inhabit a kind of hell. Theirs is a completely different world to the life you had previously lived. We often read of heads of government or top business people in Great Britain earning vast salaries and trying to justify themselves by saying that they earn every penny because of the intolerable pressure they are under. Well, I've got news for those people. I'm not saying that there isn't pressure in their jobs, because there is pressure in any job, but nobody, I repeat nobody, is under as much pressure as those kids in Calcutta, or any other Indian city where children roam the streets in their thousands. Their pressure is wondering which sewer or rubbish tip they might find a place to sleep in. Their pressure is wondering where the next bite of food is coming from and their pressure is being alone and unloved in an uncaring Indian society. That's what I call pressure, the hell of just trying to stay alive. So, you, Lottery chiefs and business executives who can't stand the pressure, retire to the golf course with your huge payoffs and thank your lucky stars because, believe me, you don't know what real pressure is. In Brazil, little kids are shot by security guards as they emerge from the sewers. That's what I call pressure and John Paul Getty had every right to fear death and reincarnation if that was what lay in store for him should he come into this world again.

As regards Albina Kujur, the news is that she has been transferred from Bihar Sharif to the convent school at Tongo, the very school she attended for all those years. She is, of course, delighted. Her life is, I suppose, a success story to inspire all Indian children born into lower caste families. She is a somebody. She seems to have settled into the teaching profession most successfully and I know that the principal, Sister Margaret Mary, is really pleased with her. I myself am proud of what she has been able to achieve through my sponsorship. She must be an inspiration to all Indian school children lucky enough to get an education. I know ActionAid no longer sponsors children at Tongo, but it does do so in many other parts of India. If anyone is interested in this kind of sponsorship after reading this book, I can tell them that I've had tremendous satisfaction from helping Albina. One of the really nice things about the *My Indian Journey* book was the many letters I've received from people saying that they were now sponsoring a child in the Third World themselves. When I get letters like that, everything becomes so worthwhile.

Albina has not mentioned the question of marriage in her letters, so I'm not sure what's going on. How could I possibly advise her about marriage? The choice must be hers. What I do know, though, is that she has worked so hard and I would hate to see her unhappy. I only hope that the decision she makes is the right one. The only advice I could give her was to think long and hard about what she wants in life. I can only assume she is doing just that.

Finally, I turn to my special friends, the Ursuline sisters of Bihar, who are spread about various parts of the state - these Divine Sisters, as I call them, who serve God and are giving an education to Indian children. I cannot thank them enough for the way they looked after me. Which ever convent school I have visited in Bihar, the sisters have been simply wonderful. How can I possibly forget them, particularly those at Tongo. I can honestly say I felt honoured to be with them and extremely fortunate to be in such illustrious company. Ursuline nuns, by their Christian nature, are such gentle human beings and of course their commitment to God is total. Their obvious happiness is evidence that they do not believe they are missing anything in their lives, and the love they give to all the school children was, for me, a joy to behold. India should be proud of those Ursuline sisters. Without them, literally thousands of children would have gone without an education.

I shall now try to give a pen portrait of each of the Divine Sisters of Tongo who I met on my second visit to the school. As I describe them, I hope my love for them shines through, because that's exactly what I feel for them.

Sister Margaret Mary: The ideal person to be principal of the school. A more charming sister I couldn't possibly have met. Loved by all her sisters and all the school children.

Sister Sarita: Extremely efficient headmistress of the senior school and a "shop steward" capable of challenging any form of officialdom - shades of Arthur Scargill!

Sister Scholastica: Headmistress of the junior school. Probably the most respected of all the sisters at Tongo and always so polite and caring.

Sister Michael: My beloved 'Auntie', who said God would be most displeased with me. She also said I'd been sent to Tongo on a mission. A wise head on her shoulders and a real character of the school, who I always felt close to.

Sister Frederic: The Florence Nightingale of the school, which was a perfect role for her. The rapport I had with her was marvellous, courtesy of her lovely sense of humour.

Sister Josephine: Now old and weary, but loved by all at Tongo. She has been excused teaching duties because of her age but is still very much part of the school.

Sister Alphonsa: My friend the cook. I literally could do no wrong in her eyes. Most concerned when I wasn't eating, she would have spoon-fed me if I'd let her.

Sister Vianney: My bodyguard, who saw to my every need. How could I have managed without her? I shall never forget the four different looks she gave me when I said I wanted to punish the chief government minister of Bihar.

Sister Harriet: The finest masseuse in all India, my very own Jewel in the Crown. In the wilds of Bihar, I'd have been in a poor way without her.

Sister Sabina: As beautiful in her ways as she was in her looks, she is the youngest sister at Tongo. God couldn't have chosen better.

Sister Armrit and Sister Terisita couldn't have been more hospitable towards me and the newer sisters at Tongo, who I'd met for the first time, made such an impression on me that I couldn't possibly fail to mention them. They are Sister Lorenza, Sister Ernesta, Sister Corula and Sister Paulina.

There are also three other Ursuline sisters who shouldn't be forgotten.

Sister Bernadette: The sister who first invited me to Tongo. Now involved in raising money for that new hospital at Gotra, which would serve 700,000 tribal people. What an achievement it will be if it becomes a reality.

Sister Angeline: The former principal of the Lohardaga Training College, who looked after Albina so very well when she was a pupil there. Her great faith and fighting spirit defeated cancer. "It's a miracle," she kept saying.

Sister Angela: The glamorous Sister Angela, of Samtoli, is the only nun I know who wears sunglasses. It was she who told me that she, along with all the other Ursuline sisters, was sworn to chastity and proud of it, too.

So, there you have it - 19 Ursuline sisters who I'm never likely to forget. And, as regards the 16 sisters at Tongo, I thank them most sincerely for making my second stay at the school such a happy one. I feel the only way I can repay them for their wonderful hospitality is to continue helping the school, so that it can become a better place. That Ursuline convent school in deepest Bihar continues to need my help. "The Golden Vision" of what that school could become is, to me, very real indeed. It reminds me so much of the film The Sound of Music, which to me recalls the innocents of India who just happen to be the most beautifully behaved school children that it's ever been my pleasure to see. The thought that they might one day sing 'Climb Every Mountain, Follow your Dream' is part and parcel of my abiding love for their country.